PUBLISHED by PARABLES
*Earthly Stories with a Heavenly Meaning*

# HUNTING
# ON THE FLY

### BY

## GLEN SOLOMON

PUBLISHED by PARABLES
Earthly Stories with a Heavenly Meaning

Hunting on the Fly
Glen Solomon

Published By Parables
December, 2019

ISBN 978-1-951497-12-5
Printed in the United States of America

Readers should be aware that Internet Web sites offered as citations and/or sources for further information may have been changed or disappeared between the time this was written and the time it is read.

# HUNTING
# ON THE FLY

## BY
## GLEN SOLOMON

PUBLISHED by PARABLES
Earthly Stories with a Heavenly Meaning

# Acknowledgements

All of these people contributed to the compilation, editing and publishing of Glen's book.

Glen Solomon, Author,
*Hunting on the Fly*

Brad Gill, Editor,
*Georgia Outdoor News*
Glen's Friend and Hunting Companion

Tyrone Hutchinson, Pastor,
Lighthouse Christian Fellowship
Glen's Pastor

John Dee Jefferies, Publisher,
Published by Parables

Daryl Kirby, Author
*Georgia Outdoor News*

Brice Nelms, Editor of the following books,
*The World Crisis and The Only Way Out*
by Jesse Hendley
*Pure Love* by Brian Peart
*Hunting on the Fly* by Glen Solomon

# Acknowledgements Continued

Bill Prince, Executive Minister,
    Biblical Principles Inc.
    Glen's Friend and Fishing Companion
    Compiler and Co-editor of *Hunting on the Fly*

Corey Solomon,
    Son of Glen Solomon

Mark Williams, Administrator,
    Satilla Outdoors
    Glen's Friend and Hunting Companion

Glen's book has been compiled and published as a ministry of Biblical Principles Inc., BPI, a 501c3 religious organization, in Hazlehurst, GA, at no cost to the owner, Cynthia Floyd Solomon, Ms. Cindy, Glen's widow. All author's profits from this book will accrue to the benefit of Ms. Cindy and no other person or organization. Any persons wanting more information concerning Glen's book or to make donations directly to Ms. Cindy can email info@biblicalprinciplesinc.org or call/text 770-313-0782.

Our prayer is that this book will be a blessing to many, as we tried to prepare it "As unto the Lord," the best we could do, in a way that Glen would like.

# Dedications

Ms. Cindy wishes to dedicate Glen's book, *Hunting on the Fly,* to the family that Glen loved so much.

Wife: Cynthia Floyd Solomon, Hazlehurst, GA

Mother-in-Law: Marilyn Floyd, Hazlehurst, GA (Prayer Warrior)

Daughter: Candace Daniels (Jeffery), Alma, GA

Son: Corey Solomon (Erica), Hazlehurst, GA

Grandson: Landon Solomon, Hazlehurst, GA

Granddaughter: Paisley Solomon, Hazlehurst, GA

Granddaughter: Madison Daniels, Alma, GA

# Table of Contents

Introduction ..........................................................................7
by Mark Williams
Prologue I: Glen Lived His Sermon Day by Day ...................12
Eulogy Delivered by Pastor Tyrone Hutchinson
Prologue II: *GON* Writer Glen Solomon Passes at 52 ...........16
Eulogy by Daryl Kirby, Author, published in the August 2019
*Georgia Outdoor News Magazine*
Chapter 1: I Am Alpha and Omega.........................................21
by Glen Solomon, with Prologue and Epilogue by Bill Prince
Chapter 2: Etiquette and Tips for WMA Hunters .................65
by Glen Solomon, published in the September 2018 *Georgia
Outdoor News Magazine*
Chapter 3: Mudfish Mayhem in the Okefenokee Swamp.....75
by Glen Solomon, published in the July 2019 *Georgia Outdoor
News Magazine*
Chapter 4: Walking Miles to Find Chickasawhatchee WMA
Hogs .....................................................................................85
by Brad Gill, published in the April 2006 *Georgia Outdoor News
Magazine,* with introduction, "Missing My Friend Glen
Solomon," by Brad Gill
Chapter 5: My Outdoor Hero................................................103
by Glen Solomon, published in the June 2016 *Georgia Outdoor
News Magazine*
Chapter 6: On the Road with Glen Solomon........................111
by Glen Solomon, published in the November 2008 *Georgia
Outdoor News Magazine*
Chapter 7: Suwannee River Warmouth................................133
by Glen Solomon, published in the May 2019 *Georgia Outdoor
New Magazine*

# Table of Contents Continued

Chapter 8: Public-Land Hog Hunting in August ................143
by Glen Solomon, published in the August 2018 *Georgia Outdoor News Magazine*

Chapter 9: *GON* Hunt Advisory Team Reports ...................155
by Glen Solomon, published in various editions of the *Georgia Outdoor News Magazine*

Chapter 10: 60 Days of Extreme WMA Hog Hunting .........161
by Glen Solomon, published in the December 2007 *Georgia Outdoor News Magazine*

Chapter 11: All Hogs and No Squirrels on Opening Day ...173
by Glen Solomon

Chapter 12: All Alone Hunting for Fort Stewart Hogs........177
by Glen Solomon, published in the August 2012 *Georgia Outdoor News Magazine*

Chapter 13: Hog Attacks Hunter on Chickasawhatchee
WMA....................................................................................185
by Glen Solomon, published in the February 2014 *Georgia Outdoor News Magazine*

Epilogue: A Celebration of the Life of Glen Solomon ........193
Eulogy Delivered by Bill Prince at Glen's Memorial Service

# Introduction

I began reading *The Georgia Outdoor News* sometime around 2011. It wasn't long after, I began to have an appreciation for one of the names I saw in the magazine on a regular basis, Glen Solomon. Not only was this man a great writer and an expert woodsman, he was also from my neck of the woods, Southeast Georgia. Glen was writing articles on hunting and fishing in some of the same areas which I frequented or were at least close by. I hoped one day to get the opportunity to meet my favorite outdoor writer. I did not realize at the time that Glen and I had actually been on several WMA hunts together without the benefit of meeting one another. DiLane Plantation was one of my favorite places to deer hunt and it was close to Glen's work at Plant Vogtle, so we were often there at the same time. Finally, Glen and I began interacting with each other on social media, beginning on October 15, 2015. It was a couple of months later that my son, Caleb, and I ran into Glen at Googe's Store in Hazlehurst. Googe's was a regular hangout for Glen, as it was a nearby hunting and fishing store where many folks sat around and told tales of the field and stream. From that meeting, we made plans to get together for a hunting trip. I cannot remember the first trip we made together, but I do believe it was at Bullard Creek WMA. From that time on, we became regular hunting and fishing partners and close friends. It is because of this time with one another that I can attest to the authenticity of the stories you are about to read. Glen Solomon was the best outdoorsman I have known. I learned as much about hunting in the short years of going with Glen as I did in the thirty years prior. Glen was at one with nature, a true nemophilist, lover of woods and forests. I stayed amazed at his knowledge of wildlife and what it took to get close to it.

*Glen Solomon slipping through a slough.*

Glen was not only an accomplished hunter but also an outstanding fisherman. He loved fishing blackwater rivers such as the Satilla, the Canoochee and the Alapaha, which are in our area. Probably his favorite body of water was the great Okefenokee Swamp. He was not only good at fishing it, but he had a love for the mystery and mystique of the Swamp. He was excited like a child at Christmas every time he got a chance to head to the Suwannee Canal or Billy's Lake. Glen knew what it took to successfully catch largemouth bass, warmouth, redbreast, and bowfin.

Glen was good at what he did because he paid attention to details that others overlooked and because of his hard work. He could decipher travel routes, bedding areas, and food sources like no one I ever hunted with. We could be walking in the woods scouting and he would suddenly stop and point out a buck's bed. I would ask questions like "Where?!" or "How do you know it was a buck?" He would then show me the ever-so-slight depression on the ground that would be bigger than an average doe and it would contain hair. Glen would palpate the bed with his bare hands to feel if it was still warm. Glen was known to go to the extreme to find and harvest game. Examples of this are things like hacking a trail with a machete down an overgrown creek in a canoe in order to get to dry land that no human had set foot on in ages, or tying smaller trees together in order to make "one" that was big enough to put a stand in, or wading in waist-deep leech-infested sloughs to get to the other side. And he would walk! Mercy at the miles we would put in on public land to get away from the people and get to the game. Glen would go through a pair of hunting boots a year. He showed no mercy to his footwear.

*Glen Solomon with a big boar.*

Glen also kept several notebooks full of GPS coordinates. If he lost his GPS or bought a new one, he had his endless list of coordinates with which to start again. His GPS was a part of him. He also kept a collection of WMA maps. I was even with him once on a new WMA when he "re-drew" the DNR map because it was not accurate. He said, "That road is not there. It's over here and turns this way." Then, he would make the correction on the paper map. I asked him, "Glen, are you surveying the entire piece of property?" He said, "Well, how else am I going to learn it?" And learn it he did. I doubt there is another human being, past or present, that was as familiar with South Georgia WMAs as was Glen Solomon. You could not hear him give directions to a particular area on a WMA without being astounded. He knew every split oak tree, hollow, and ditch. He hunted on the fly. Always going somewhere different. But never out of state. He said he had all he could handle right here in Georgia.

Glen was an outstanding and well accomplished hunter and fisherman. But he was also a godly family man and friend. He loved the outdoors but that came behind his love for his Lord, his family, and his friends. He was a friend to many and always took time to share his knowledge. He will be missed, but his stories and memories will be around for years to come. I hope you enjoy this collection of his stories as much as I have.

Mark Williams
Administrator, Satilla Outdoors

# Prologue I:
## Glen Lived His Sermon Day by Day
(Eulogy delivered by Glen's Pastor, Rev. Tyrone Hutchinson at Glen's Memorial Service)

*"For all flesh is as grass, and all the glory of man as the flower of grass. The grass withereth, and the flower thereof falleth away"* (1 Peter 1:24, KJV).

*"Go to now, ye that say, Today or tomorrow we will go into such a city, and continue there a year, and buy and sell, and get gain: Whereas ye know not what shall be on the morrow. For what is your life? It is even a vapour, that appeareth for a little time, and then vanisheth away. For that ye ought to say, If the Lord will, we shall live, and do this, or that"* (James 4:13-15, KJV).

*"As for man, his days are as grass: as a flower of the field, so he flourisheth. For the wind passeth over it, and it is gone; and the place thereof shall know it no more"* (Psalm 103:15-16, KJV).

*"Man that is born of woman is of few days, and full of trouble. He cometh forth like a flower, and is cut down: he fleeth also as a shadow, and continueth not"* (Job 14:1-2, KJV).

All these verses talk to us about the uncertainty of our tomorrows. When brother Glen started out hog hunting Friday morning, I don't believe he considered that would be his final day in this life. He finished his hunt and experienced pain. Then driving himself to the hospital, he kept wife Cindy on the phone until arriving there at the emergency center where he passed away.

None of us know what another day will bring for our lives. That's why we should make our calling and election sure in the Lord! I believe Brother Glen Solomon had made his calling sure and steadfast. We really can't preach anyone else's funeral sermon. We live our sermons. We create our testimonies, our sermons, by the way we live. I feel honored to participate in this service today, but I must remind us that Brother Glen preached his own message!...As we all do.

He did that each Sunday morning coming here to worship and honor God. He did that responding and coming forward in prayer. His place of prayer was about here. (*Pastor Ty pointed to a place on the altar.*) He did that in loving and leading his family in worship. He preached by example living and walking with God. He preached his sermon through his gentle and kind spirit. Glen was Glen wherever you saw him - the same! His sermon, his message, said to me, he loved his family, his church, and certainly his God and he worshipped Him unashamedly.

Someone said of Glen, he was loveable, likeable, easy to get along with and a friendly guy. In living his sermon, I never heard him raise his voice in anger, or say anything critical of others or spread a rumor about anyone. A part of his sermon of life was related to and had to do with his love for the outdoors, hunting and fishing and enjoying nature at its best. Now I like to hunt and fish, but Glen was a master

13

of both. He kept his freezer stocked with venison, pork and fish. At a church supper you could always count on some wild game being served from Glen. He was pictured recently with a stringer of fish in a magazine of some sort. Glen actually wrote articles and stories for hunting and fishing periodicals. He was a writer and a good one.

Another thing about Glen you have to admire, he never bragged about his catch! Most of us would never stop telling our story if we caught fish like he did, but not Glen!

All the scriptures I shared today point us to how brief life really is! How uncertain our tomorrows are! Learning of Brother Glen's passing, I began to question, how could this be? Just 52 years old, appeared to be very healthy, very active, enjoyed outdoor activities. No known signs of failing health and just suddenly he is gone. How, God, could this be? But wait a moment! What if Brother Glen had fallen sick, suffering, degenerating with some dread disease? Would suffering, dying a long, drawn-out death, would that have been better? Would this have pleased him, his family and friends? I don't think so! We miss Glen and will miss him as days come and go, but Glen was doing what he loved and enjoyed and what made up a part of his life! Then, without a lengthy sickness and drawn-out suffering, he answered his call and went to be with Jesus.

Knowing Brother Glen and his passion for living and his love for God, let's redirect our questions and sorrows toward God in worship, praise and thanksgiving for his life well-lived and let us determine to live our lives for the glory of God. Keep singing, worshipping, praising and praying. Keep Glen's story and his sermon of life alive through sharing experiences, testimonials, and his love for life, the examples he left us. Determine to build on his good examples, his legacy, and make a great example for others to follow.

Again, remembering our scripture today on the brevity of life, let's take a look at our lives, consider our relationship with Jesus, make sure and certain our relationship with Jesus so that we know when our appointment comes, we will be ready to meet Jesus!

*"For God so loved the world, that He gave his only begotten Son, that whosoever believeth in Him should not perish, but have everlasting life"* (John 3:16, KJV).

*"If we confess our sins, He is faithful and just to forgive us our sins, and to cleanse us from all unrighteousness"* (1 John 1:9, KJV).

*"That if thou will confess with thy mouth the Lord Jesus, and shalt believe in thine heart that God hath raised him from the dead, thou shalt be saved"* (Romans 10:9, KJV).

Rev. Tyrone Hutchinson - August 18, 2019

# Prologue II:
## GON Writer Glen Solomon Passes At 52

By Daryl Kirby
Published by *GON*, August 2019

*GON* writer Glen Solomon, 52, of Hazlehurst, passed away on Friday, Aug. 16 while on his way to Appling Health Care in Baxley with what he told his wife over the phone were chest pains.

Visitation and funeral services were held Sunday, Aug. 18 at Lighthouse Christian Fellowship in Hazlehurst, Glen's home church.

Glen's relationship with *GON* began in November 2005, when he first met *GON* Editor Brad Gill at Chickasawhatchee WMA. Brad was featuring Glen and his public-land hog-hunting techniques. From that hunt, a work relationship flourished, and Glen began writing stories for *GON* in January 2007. His initial story was called, "60 Days of Extreme WMA Hog Hunting," and the title certainly sums up Glen's extreme passion for not only Georgia hunting and fishing but sharing it with a large fan base of readers.

Also on the Chickasawhatchee hog hunt with Glen and Brad were Glen's good friend Don Wood and Glen's son, Corey. Corey posted the below message on Facebook on Saturday, Aug. 17, the day after his father's passing:

*Glen was able to take this Big Hammock WMA hog just a few hours before his passing on Friday, Aug. 16. After shooting the hog, he took the time to video how to bone it out on the ground, something he desired to share with his GON and social-media fans.*

"I wanted to take a moment to fill everyone in on the situation as I sit out here in the woods talking to my dad and the Lord. Dad went by himself yesterday morning to Big Hammock WMA to hunt hogs on the second day of small game. Upon leaving, he called my mother and told her that he was having chest pains, and he was driving himself to the hospital. My mother was on the phone with him the entire trip. He drove himself all the way to the Baxley hospital where he fell unconscious as soon as he arrived, and mom filled in the nurses, who got to him as soon as he arrived. They were never able to bring him back.

"The cause of death was ruled as a blood clot that traveled into his lungs. Heart attack and stroke were ruled out. We are all still in shock as reality hasn't set in yet. He will be greatly missed by all of us, as well as a lot of you guys. Thank you all for being great friends and fans of his. He truly adored all of you and your comments. And also, here is one more gift from him to us all. Upon picking up his truck, I looked in his cooler and there was a fresh, boned-out hog from the morning hunt. And while checking his phone, we found the pictures of the hog, along with an instruction video he made of how to bone one out on the ground just for you guys. Please pray for my family and his friends in this time."

The picture of Glen and his hog is included in this article and the video of how to bone-out a hog on the ground are on Glen's Facebook page. The last video news story Glen did for *GON* was when he interviewed Kristen Peterson after she caught a 16-lb. bass.

Glen will not only be missed by a number of fans who enjoyed opening their *GON* and reading about what Glen was hunting or catching, but he had a great group of friends who enjoyed "Hunting on the Fly" with him, a technique of running from one WMA or public fishing hole to the next and collecting game and fish for the freezer.

"My heart is broken," said Mark Williams, a close friend to Glen and his family. "The man who has taught me so much about life in the woods and water and life in the home and in the Lord was called to his heavenly home.

"All that was said at the funeral was good and uplifting about Glen and the life he lived. There was a lot of good to be said by him. There was no shortage of material for a eulogy.

"Glen was a Godly man, he was a funny man, he was a passionate man. He was a good friend to a lot of people, a close friend to a lot of people, even people who hadn't even met him yet. He influenced their life in a big way."

*Glen was known as a funny man. Here, he takes a little different approach to encourage folks to take a kid hunting. The young lady in the bag is his granddaughter, Paisley.*

According to the Wainright-Parlor Funeral Home in Hazlehurst, Glen is preceded in death by his grandmother,

"Ma" Jurell Solomon, mother, Patsy Anderson Solomon, and brother, Greg Solomon.

Survivors include his wife, Cindy Floyd Solomon of Hazlehurst; daughter, Candace Daniels (Jeffery) of Alma; son, Corey Solomon (Erica) of Hazlehurst; father, Wayne Solomon of Douglas; Aunt Frances Vickers of Ambrose; half-sisters, Latrice Solomon of Chauncey and Michelle Carter of Ponte Vedra Beach, FL; half-brother, Wade Pritchard of Douglas; three grandchildren, Landon Solomon, Paisley Solomon, Madison Daniels, nieces and nephews also survived.

# Chapter 1
## I Am Alpha and Omega

CHAPTER 1 PROLOGUE by Bill Prince

This is a prologue to Chapter 1 of Hunting on the Fly, a book by Glen Solomon. It was around mid-June, 2019, when Glen Solomon gave me a manuscript for a book he was writing. He wanted me to evaluate his progress and possibly to help him get it published. I have been a writer of short stories for many years, some of which have been published online. I also have been an editor of two books which the organization for which I am executive has successfully published. As I read the manuscript, I was not surprised to conclude quickly that it should be published because I knew that Glen Solomon was a gifted writer. There were sentences and paragraphs in the manuscript that were crying out to be published. I tested a couple paragraphs on my wife, reading them to her aloud. These were descriptions of hunting scenarios that Glen had written. She is not now and never has been a hunter of any game, yet she said that she understood the situations perfectly that Glen had written about and that she could see them playing out in her mind as I read the words that Glen had laced together into sentences and then paragraphs. Consequently, with that confirmation, I decided that I would assist Glen in publishing his manuscript, which was then entitled, *I Am Alpha and Omega*.

When I got the first inkling that something was wrong with Glen on the morning of August 16, it was very disturbing and just shortly later I learned of his untimely death. I thought immediately many things relating to Glen and our relationship as friends and sportsmen, and of the reading I was doing of the manuscript. It did not take long for a plan to develop, whereby I would push forward with the concept of publishing Glen's manuscript; the text quality of which I thought to be excellent however, the quantity of which was almost eleven thousand words and was insufficient to create a book for which we would ideally need at least forty-five thousand words and possibly as many as sixty thousand. As I prayed for Glen's widow, Ms. Cindy and Glen's children and grandchildren, an idea formed, I believe born of God, that we could lace together more of Glen's writings to supplement "I Am Alpha and Omega" to the point where we would have a sufficient amount of Glen's writings of which a wonderful book would consist. Approximately the first of September, I shared the God-inspired concept for this book with Ms. Cindy and Glen's son Corey and of course, they gave me encouragement to proceed. As I write this prologue to "I Am Alpha and Omega," the team that came together to assemble Glen's Book is almost done. It is now almost Halloween and we hope to have it out by Thanksgiving. At the close of Chapter One of Glen's book, *Hunting on the Fly*, I will add an epilogue which I believe will be additional proof to people of faith in Christ that this book is indeed the fruit of Glen's faith and produced as the will of God. This Chapter One, "I Am Alpha and Omega," led us into a book that will be a God-inspired part of Glen's legacy, a God-provided asset for Ms. Cindy, and a joy to her family and fans of Glen Solomon everywhere.

## I AM ALPHA AND OMEGA
By Glen Solomon

"I AM ALPHA AND OMEGA THE FIRST AND THE LAST: AND WHAT THOU SEEST, WRITE IN A BOOK..."
(Revelation 1:11, KJV).

and that's exactly what I did, here it is...

JAN 11, 2010. My good friend David Rodriguez of Homestead, Florida and I headed out to the Pataula Creek tract of Lake Walter F. George WMA for an evening bow hunt. Little did I know what an adventure, physical and emotional, this trip would bring. Last December, along the beautiful hardwood ridges of this Chattahoochee River impoundment, I'd taken two mature bucks, an 8-point I rattled in and a 10 point that's no longer teased by a certain flashy doe. I was eager for another chance to stab an arrow before season ran out in the next few days. Until now, I hadn't got a chance to hunt here this season due to work travel and the holiday seasons. Being today was 1/11, I wanted to succeed even more. And here's the lengthy explanation for that last comment.

The number 111 has been shockingly prevalent in my family's life for the last couple years and continues to be so.

It always accompanies something good and regularly, as a confirmation, when right decisions have been made. I will cover just a few occurrences of hundreds to show what I mean. It's hard to fathom the multitude of this sign that has been present in our everyday lives and the realization it has come from GOD. We felt the HOLY SPIRIT many times concurring with 111. It's awesome!

*Young Glen with an 8-point.*

What is it? Is it part of something bigger? A step towards a culmination of things building for the future?

GOD said he would give HIS people clues. Buddy, I believe it now! All I know it's present too much in our everyday lives to be luck. We never look for it on purpose and it'll pop up in a nonchalant manner. It's weird how it's never 1:10 or 1:12 or $1.10 or $1.12. It may be 111 on a mile marker post, a billboard, a vehicle tag or a phone number. Again, not purposefully looking for it, it will have exact timing with a moment of decision or a choice of something, helping to direct us on the right path. It will accompany a good thing precisely before it happens or right thereafter, or both. I wish I'd kept accurate records of all these instances that 111 has hit, especially at such opportune moments in life. But initially, I never dreamed it would be so often. I'm afraid if I'd shared with others, they would coldly shun it as someone talking about some "lucky number," as some of you may be thinking that now. I can assure you it's not that. Throughout the BIBLE, you will note GOD has used certain numbers frequently, especially the number 7 and the triple digits of Satan, the Great Deceiver of many. I believe the number 111 is a clue and part of a mechanism that GOD has applied to my family, that strengthens our walk with HIM. I know my family and I are blessed and uplifted each time we read this. It could be that this writing is not to be shared and just used for our blessing and reassurance. But, I haven't been led to keep it secret. Yet, I have let very few read this, primarily for the reason it may be taken wrong, being a number and all. Maybe HE has been giving you clues along and along, but in a different form or fashion. Ask HIM through prayer and you may see yours.

It all started when my mother-in-law, Marilyn Floyd, woke up late one night, which hardly ever happens. That night she awoke from a deep slumber. Immediately looking at the clock, thinking it was time to get up with the chickens, she noticed it was only 1:11 a.m. Upon awakening, she felt the HOLY SPIRIT come over her. Usually when that happens and especially at such an odd hour, she senses who or what to pray for. But this time it was strangely different, only feeling a strong focus for the time, 1:11. Amazingly the next two nights at exactly 1:11, she was awakened again! She prayed, "LORD, if this is of you, have me to awake at this time again." Well, the fourth night in a row, she again awoke from a deep sleep. Guess what time? Yep, 1:11! Confusingly, she still received no thought of a directional subject for prayer, just HIS strong presence with each late-night visit at that exact time. Marilyn, Granny as we call her, is definitely the enduring prayer warrior of our family, so when she spoke of this, we were quick to listen. We wondered, "What is it? Is something to happen on that date? A sign of sorts?" It wasn't long before 111 was showing up nearly every day, not just as a time on a device but numerous other ways. And strangely at exact times I mentioned earlier. Here are a few examples.

A week after Granny's dream was actually the first time I noticed 111 had a role in giving me confirmation that I did the right thing. I got involved in a major work issue that led me to quit after I voiced an opinion rather strongly on behalf of my work crew. I was right to do so, but with the upper management of this company degraded and embarrassed before their customer, which really showed their ignorance and uncaring of our safety concerns, I decided to quit before I got fired. Our crew balked and "blew the whistle" on this certain issue that had been affecting and jeopardizing workers' health and welfare at this site for decades. No one before had stood up to this huge contractor and corporate giant, but our crew did, with me compiling information from the exposed workers and creating a 22-page document. The biggest threat to them wasn't from any regulatory agencies (it's a dirty world out there), but the threat and exposure of going to the media which would give some powerful ammo to certain lobbyists who are fighting daily to end the new plant construction of this type of industry. Too many billions at stake for one plant to give the whole global industry a black eye. In the end, they quit the manipulation of covering up safety concerns, became more stringent on following the proper work practices and listened diligently to all future safety concerns of the workers. I'm sure due to our period of involvement that some lives were saved and others extended because of this silent killer.

After leaving this job site, I wrote a personal documentation of my account, but it quickly snow-balled beyond that, turning into a plant-wide event after my old crew members and others who were exposed, also wanted a copy for their future reference. While meeting with several of them, they started adding their own experiences and concerns dealing with this fiasco. The documentation started growing daily with amendments and grievances as I met with many after their shifts had ended, day and night. Thereafter, nightly I was awakened by the HOLY SPIRIT to type out more literature for the documentation. Boy, would the words flow! Between the daily and nightly conferences, strange people following me, the worry of no income for looming bills, and nightly sessions on the keyboard, I had only gotten a few hours of sleep in over a week. Yet, I felt rested and refreshed as if I had ample sleep every night because HE was in control!

I dealt with a corporate investigator during this time. After hanging up with him after a very satisfying phone conversation dealing with the proposed remedies and solutions for our grievances and demands for the future, I noticed the page blinking on my cell phone. Flashing was the duration of our call, 1 hour and 11 minutes! Along with the last 3 digits of his phone number, *111! Immediately, I felt the HOLY SPIRIT from head to toe! Ashamedly, I haven't felt it in a long time and it felt really good. I even prayed, "Is this of YOU?" HE hit me again with that inner warm feeling of love and a sensation of hugging arms. Also, I had chill bumps of a very different kind, not cold but lasting much longer, building up into such intensity that it permeates your soul. You can definitely identify that the Soul exists when the HOLY SPIRIT enters you. It's apparent as the fingers on your hand! It was a while before the hairs on my neck settled, not from being scared, but from knowing HE was present! Even though I had drifted back into being a "good ole boy" since I was saved in 1987, I had back-slidden from the Christian I was the first couple years after being reborn. However, today I still consider myself a daily work in progress, striving to be the Christian I need and want to be. It's hard, but I can do it with the GREAT HELPER!

After the above turmoil subsided, GOD quickly took care of my needs.

*"But my GOD shall supply all your needs according to his riches in glory by Christ Jesus"* (Philippians 4:19, KJV).

*"Therefore take no thought, saying, What shall we eat? or, What shall we drink? or, Wherewithal shall we be clothed? For all these*

*things do the Gentiles seek: for your heavenly Father knoweth that ye have need of all these things: But seek ye first the kingdom of GOD, and his righteousness, and all these things shall be added unto you"* (Matthew 6:31-33, KJV).

I landed another job in Maryland that is nearly impossible to get unless you know the "right" person. The next two jobs I went to were in Pennsylvania and Texas, which are even harder to get in. I left home for Maryland with a relieving inner peace and a smile. The phone number for the business agent that called that day ended in 111. When I arrived in Texas for that job, the proprietor placed me in room 111. Confirmation before and after! It was the best run I've ever had for a spring work season. HE can lead you from the dark and into the light, on HIS time!

*"Thy word is a lamp unto my feet, and a light unto my path"* (Psalm 119:105).

My son Corey took a licensing exam that would move him up to a higher pay scale and position at his job. We prayed for his success as a family, believing and claiming together in HIS name. Where two or more come together in HIS name, there will HE be also! He took the very challenging test and passed, even without having time to study. Later when visiting in Texas, Corey showed us his license certificate. I noticed the date he took it was on 1/11 and under "fees paid," $111.00!

Cindy and I fished in a bass tournament trail for couples. On the one tournament we placed in, 111 was present beforehand. The night before the tourney, we checked into a motel. Strangely, the clerk gave us a handicapped room, even though the place had very few folks staying at it. Reckon the clerk seen something about me I didn't? Haha! Guess what room number! Yep, 111! I told Cindy, "We're gonna do good tomorrow!" Well, we placed 3rd the next day, our only money place on the trail that season. In my heart, I knew we were destined to win, but I blew it. We had a little spat about something hormonal an hour before weigh-in, while trying to dredge out our last keeper for a full limit. In my anger, I made a profane remark. I immediately felt very dark inside. In the next few minutes along a line of docks, I lost 3 bass right at the boat, spitting my flipping tube out just as I went to lip them. Any which of the three would've won the tournament for us. I was given that little test HE gives us sometimes right before we are rewarded, and I failed. But GOD is a gracious GOD, still allowing us to place in a very grueling tournament. Just think, how far can we go in our Christian lives if we don't give into bad habits, especially when GOD is steering? Don't make HIM pull off onto the shoulder every time you face a curve in life, you'll never get to where you need to be in life and as a Christian. Next season, we got a "Big Fish" award after seeing another 111.

After the Christmas holidays, my son and his family had a 15-hour trip back to Texas. Before leaving, we prayed together for GOD'S traveling mercy upon the road. On the way back, somewhere in the spaghetti junction of roads in a metropolitan area, he got lost, setting him back an hour or so. He finally stopped and asked for directions at a store. While there he purchased some drinks and snacks. The cashier rang up, $11.11! Confirmation GOD had directed and re-timed his path for a reason HE knew. Always pray for GOD'S mercies on your travels, short or long. To this day, when I travel long distances to and from work sites, the first number that I notice anywhere, being a car tag or whatever, is 111. And no, I don't look for it on purpose, like I mentioned earlier. If I believed in "lucky" numbers and other superstitions, I'd pray for all black cats to stay off the road too! I do continue to pray with my family before leaving to job sites and on speakerphone when returning and before entering America's most dangerous place, the highway.

Working in Virginia, I had to stay at a distant motel an hour drive away. I had to put up with a lot of congested traffic and the general area was really crime-infested. Cindy was with me, so I stayed at one that had constant security. Fifteen hours a day, including the daily commute, was beginning to take a toll on me. There was only one affordable motel near the plant and unless you put in a reservation a year ahead, it's almost impossible to get a room there. They also keep a lengthy waiting list in case someone cancels or leaves early. I didn't reserve accordingly, as I've never worked this area before. I had a friend staying there who kept checking on a room periodically even though I wasn't on the list. On my day off, Cindy and I was sitting at a traffic light downtown. I spoke to Cindy, "I wish I could get a room over there. I could get a lot more rest and save a lot on gas too." I also knew I could carpool and leave her with a way to go. Cheaper rates, no worrying about getting mugged or approached by deadbeats as it was on the outskirts of a much smaller city than the huge metropolis across the James River Bridge. Exactly after I made that wishful comment, Cindy said, "Look at the bus sitting at the other light. See the number across the top of the windshield?" I mouthed the words "111" and the phone rang. It was my friend Dale saying, "Hey, you still want a room over here? They have an opening." Thank GOD! This call also came on my one day off, making moving more convenient. HE is the MASTER PLANNER!

Here are a few memories that show GOD is my frequent hunting partner, the best one I could ever ask for. At a recent outdoor ministry I attended, pastor Jeff Hines of Fort Gaines said, "GOD wants to be your EVERYTHING in your EVERYTHING!" We've all heard people say they would do the GOD thing later, figuring they would have to give up all pursuits, such as hunting and fishing, time in the outdoors, etc. and thus, no time to "holy roll" on a street corner 24/7. Boy, are they confused! People need to realize GOD wants and needs to be included in Everything, walking within you 24/7. HE didn't say quit life and stop doing things you enjoy, as long as they're not of a sinful nature and not to put those pursuits before HIM. HE can rid you of those sinful pursuits and enhance the good ones, but everything in priority. HE'S there to help. HE died on the cross for you. Say the sinner's prayer and never look back. Those sins and your sinful nature will be washed away and forgotten, and you will start anew.

*"For GOD so loved the world, that he gave his only begotten Son, that whosoever believeth in him should not perish, but have everlasting life,"* (John 3:16, KJV).

*"Wash me thoroughly from mine iniquity, and cleanse me from my sin"* (Psalm 51:2, KJV).

I usually average a couple dozen or more game animals a year as my family and I choose to live off the land as much as possible. GOD provided us with a bountiful and renewable resource.

*"Every moving thing that liveth shall be meat for you; even as the green herb have I given you all things"* (Genesis 9:3, KJV).

Since the recognition of 111, and nearly all my kills since then, 111 was present before, after or both. That's a lot of 111's cause we eat lots of critters. They are not coincidences. Coincidences don't have a pattern of reliability at precise moments.

*"In whom also we have obtained an inheritance, being predestinated according to the purpose of him who worketh all things after the counsel of his own will,"* (Ephesians 1:11, KJV).

During the summer, I hog hunt a lot beginning August 15ᵗʰ, when the WMA's open. I do a lot of walking, averaging 3-6 miles a day and have been up to 12 miles in one day. I have a lot to check out after 30 years of experience on over three dozen public lands scattered around half the state. Of course I don't cover that many every year, but do hit and run as many as possible, depending on how each subsequent area produces. I have several hundred waypoints stored on my GPS and I burn a lot of boot leather implementing those waypoints in a process of elimination until I find them. What if I made the same number of steps doing something for the LORD all those years? OUCH!

*Glen with small boar.*

These waypoint descriptions include hot spots such as main trails and junctions, wallows, bedding/security areas, islands in flooded swamps, and sanctuaries during times of heavy hunting pressure. After I pull up and park at a certain location, I fire up the GPS and start laying out a "connect-the-dot" trail. I'll usually work an elliptical or figure-eight pattern, going and coming back on different routes. As I scroll down through the list of waypoints, their respective distances will be displayed, beginning with the nearest. I've lost count of how many that noted 1.11 miles. I then completely disregard all the others, trashing my connect-the-dot battle plan. I gather my gear for the long hike and take off to that one far destination, eager to see what awaits me. I have been successful every time! I repeat, every time! This has also happened on a few deer hunts. Showing my degree of confidence, I would call Cindy and tell her, "I'm fixin' to get sumpin!" thus claiming my victory through JESUS, even beforehand. Many times after bagging game while working my C-T-D strategy or pilfering around in a new area, I would hit the GPS for the most direct route back to the truck so I could quickly get the quartered meat on ice, it would read "1.11 miles!" Down to my knees again, praising HIM for the confirmation.

I'm glad I gave my Everything to HIM. Of upmost importance it needs to be your heart, then your family, then work your way down the list even to things you may consider too small. Like pastor Benny Tate says, "Do you think anything is too big for GOD?" Shouldn't GOD be your constant companion in all things, not just calling on HIM when it's "woe on me?"

The fall of 2010, I got called in for an outage job a little earlier than normal, which would cut out most of my bow season. I really wanted some other plants to call first that would have better schedules to accommodate my hunting schedule. One plant in mind would be having a later outage, allowing me to hunt the first part of bow season and I'd also be back for the remaining majority of gun season. The other hopeful option was near my place on Lake Eufaula, where I do most of my bowhunting anyhow, thus allowing more time in the woods.

But GOD had other plans. During family prayer, we always pray about the "right" job. So, when I get a call, that's where I go. Even though I sign up for several places around the nation, I rely on HIS Wisdom to direct my paths. Glen (me) doesn't always knows what's best for Glen, but GOD does! HE can open and close the right doors to direct those paths, and because of our stubbornness, use stumbling blocks if need be. A few years ago, my job decisions were strongly influenced by hunting and fishing, having life's priorities backwards for most of my adult life. I finally grew up at forty-something, well...mostly. I put that there in case my wife reads this. I love to see her happy, laughing and all. Since praying for GOD to direct my work paths, many jobs I went to were not my first choice or where I thought I needed to be. In the end, I ALWAYS found out why it was the best choice.

Unknowingly at the time, accepting this particular job created the perfect timing to land the next one, a plant I've never worked, and the best money-maker I've ever been on. AMEN! The phone rang at 1:11, and without any hesitation, I accepted the job offer even though it wasn't the one I'd hoped for. Yet, I was glad because HE has never been wrong!

GOD is a Gracious GOD, too. Surprisingly, I was able to obtain hunting privileges on plant property. There were a few deer, not many but at least somewhere I could hunt on my one day off. Grabbing my bow and heading out that first day, I glanced at the microwave while closing the door behind me. The time was never set, and of course, off by a few hours. The time said, "1:11." I immediately felt the HOLY SPIRIT's whisper. Some people may call that their "little voice" or a pulsating instinct. Not so, mine has a name, the capital letters you just read.

I called my wife en route to the woods and told her about the great evening I was about to have. I knew nothing about the approximate 80-acre tract, so I threw my climber on my back and walked until I found something promising. Finally, after two hours of speed-scouting and sweating profusely in mid-September heat, I found a scraggly persimmon tree at the far corner of the long rectangular-shaped block, 3/4 of a mile from the truck. A couple of persimmons were knocked down from last night's winds when a thunderstorm passed through. A few minutes before dark, I looked down through the pines and spotted a lone doe weaving among the trees, apparently working the evening thermals as she looped in from my downwind position in the treetops. Forty yards and still good. C'mon girl, a little closer. 30, 25, Hey, I may have a chance! Stance ready, full draw. Mental checks in place. Aha! I straightened my form, eased my bow back up and aimed directly out from my level. I made the mistake of many, by following the deer in and dropping my bow arm, thus I changed my form and line of sight. Fifteen yards, I bent at the waist, bringing the bow back on target. As the doe curled around the last sapling and turning broadside, I let out a barely audible short bleat, maa... THWAACK! She blasted out to 28 yards, looked around for a couple seconds, then did a little teetering, PLOP! Awesome! Falling within sight after a perfect and clean hit is definitely one of the many ecstasies of bowhunting.

However, the best feeling is kneeling down besides your trophy and while stroking and laying your hand on its hide, begin praising and sharing your harvest with the CREATOR, the one HE provided. On my knees in GOD'S Great Outdoors with tears running down my face with HIS presence enshrouding you is a feeling that you will never forget, nor duplicate! I also feel a very deep and enriched sense of tradition, knowing that many others before have praised HIM for their blessed hunts. All the way back to the time of Esau fulfilling the wish of his dying father.

*"Now therefore take, I pray thee, thy weapons, thy quiver and thy bow, and go out to the field, and take me some venison"* (Genesis 27:3, KJV).

*"Bring me venison, and make me savoury meat, that I may eat, and bless thee before the LORD before my death"* (Genesis 27:7, KJV).

*Glen tired and sitting with a spike buck.*

The next week, I climbed super early on the same open pine ridge, positioned along a dim trail that I assumed the deer were using to access what I guesstimated to be the only possible bedding area on the property, a small thicket of wild plums. It was fairly open terrain with an old two path cutting across it, which I was adjacent to from my perch in the pines. When I got settled in, I checked the sunrise app on my GPS to verify legal shooting light and to calculate how long my wait, or rest for that matter, would be until then. Guess how long? Yep, 1 hour and 11 minutes!

Shortly after daybreak, scanning the two-path which ran uphill through the middle of the pines, I spotted two deer crossing at the crest of it. I immediately grunted, using my voice. The doe in front paused, then turned toward me and started trotting down the path. The little basket-racked buck that was trailing behind, watched her be-bop on down the road for a few seconds until he couldn't stand it any longer. "Wait for me!" The doe turned broadside onto the trail that passed by my tree at 16 yards. A low bleat stopped her in mid-stride. I saw the spiraling single white vane of my arrow drill snugly behind the crease of her shoulder. THUUMP! The arrow hit so hard, the two legs on that side lifted so high it mocked the onset of a full body slam. With the two legs tilted, and the others getting lower in a half-circle run, the deer piled up within 15 yards. Wow!

Just before the thwang of the bow string, the 7-point trailing behind a few yards, hit my scent pool, "turnt innered out" and shot back up the hill, much quicker than he came down it. Stopping at the crest 80 yards away, he looked back my way, seeming a little reluctant to leave. Apparently, the doe was in heat, so I mustered out a long mewling estrus bleat. Must've sounded sexy enough. He come bouncing back down the hill like a pronghorn antelope. Actually though, he looked more like Tigger, BOING! BOING! BOING! He knew exactly where she turned off and could see the white of her belly, but I could tell by his speed he wasn't going to stop and turn onto the trail, knowing something 'hanky" was going on. He looked kinda funny with his rotating head swiveling harder to the left with each bounce while his body carried straight ahead down the road. Cruising by like a rubber-necker past the scene of the incident, I had to give him plenty of lead. It's good I had a big peep with a single pin setup. Everything centered, front of the brisket, a release of the caliper, a streak of carbon shaft.....psssst....THUNK! He rocketed out of there so quick he nearly left his antlers behind! I looked to my arrow, now sunk deep in the pine needles where his shadow had been a moment ago. I mentioned a single white vane earlier. I didn't see one now among the other two orange ones, but three darkened ones. AMEN!! I decided to give the buck a little time, as the hit looked to be a little back, but still lung.

*Glen with a big 8-point.*

An hour later, 150 yards away, while kneeling on a carpet of pine needles and face lifted above, I was able again to give that same praising prayer of success, a third time! I found the buck propped up against a sycamore, seemingly in a ready pose. I took the photo just like he lay. THANK YOU, JESUS!

Isn't GOD good! I'd done wrote off getting to bow hunt any, but HE made the means for me and my family to obtain some much-needed venison that will surely hide the bottom of our freezer, thanks to HIS replenishing bounty. I was off three days that outage, hunting only two of them and killed three. The one day I didn't hunt during my last week there, Plant Security had called and left a message on my phone, saying that my privileges had been revoked. They stated that hunting on plant property was for permanent employees, not temps. Strange, as other temps have been hunting out there for years and told me how to apply. Security's mistake since they approved the application. Some of the questions on the app were, "Are you a permanent or a temporary employee? If not permanent, what contractor?" All answers were answered correctly and truthfully. The approving officer said, "Here's your pass and maps. Log in and out each day. Good luck!" What truly happened in this case is that GOD guided the hand that stamped "APPROVED" across the front of the application. HE is the MASTER PLANNER!

Later that winter, my son Corey was down for the Christmas holidays. Loving to hunt also, his fever was high as he has nowhere to hunt in Texas nor any public land nearby either. At the time, I was only hunting public land and had no private land access, at least none that could provide a decent chance for a deer. He only had a morning or two he could go while here, but with the added cost of a WMA stamp, it was too costly for only a couple chances. Besides, the only two WMA's open were nearly two hours away and the hunting was fair at best.

During that time, a work friend of mine, Royce Pierce of Lyons, of whom I'd met only a few months ago, called to chat with me. When we got to the subject of deer hunting (which doesn't take long for two South Georgia rednecks), I explained my son's dilemma of wanting to hunt but because of short notice, short money, and the distance to travel to anything open, it wasn't feasible nor very appealing to do so. Royce said, "Shoot, that ain't a problem, come over here by the house. I just got permission on a new piece of land." Talk about perfect timing! Corey said, it would mean a lot to sky up a tall pine and watch the Georgia woods come alive. It'd be a far cry from the Dallas metro area.

We were to meet Royce at a convenience store early the next morning and follow him out to the property. An hour after arriving at our chosen time, Royce still hadn't shown. I made a call and a text, with no response. Corey was visibly getting upset, wanting the day to start off right and seeing his one golden opportunity possibly slipping away. I tried to encourage him, explaining from past experiences of playing this game a long time, many of my days that started off wrong or bad turned out to be some of my best days afield. You have to stay confident and never give up. Royce finally called and said he'd overslept and he'd be right on, if we still wanted to go, being it was already broad daylight. I said, "Sure c'mon." After arriving, he explained that he'd only gotten a couple hours sleep due to getting called into work on an emergency, and being wore slap out, didn't hear the alarm clock.

We got to the woods, knelt and said a prayer for our safety and success and took off into strange territory. Royce was also new to the area, but his dad had recently pre-scouted it, describing a location to him along a dim two-path road where a hardwood branch met it at a curve. Across the road was some real thick regenerative growth, which would most likely be the bedding and security area for the deer. I noticed Royce looking for a certain tree his dad further described, to be the one he needed to climb. It needed to be the right one among several to be able to see a major deer trail among the tall bushes and saplings. He figured it out and Corey quickly scaled 40 foot up the slash pine. It was well past daylight and the sun was up in the air, burning off the remaining shadows of dawn. I wonder if Royce could've found that tree in the dark and on the correct side of the curve in the road? I doubt it. Hmmm... GOD'S Plan? I know so!

Around 10:45, all of us with commanding majestic views from a towering pine, a shot rang out. From a distance, I could see Corey fidgeting in his climber. I radioed him with the two-way. He informed me, "I shot the last of three does after watching 'em a few minutes. They were staging near the road before coming out of the thick stuff!" I rejoiced inside, "Hallelujah!" Within the minute, my cell phone vibrated. I figured it was Royce wanting to know who shot, and what. The text displayed was, " Call me on my work phone, this one is dying. The number is ***- *111. Whoa! The HOLY SPIRIT came over me in a rush and tears welled up. AMEN! Confirmation again from a great GOD who had been our silent hunting partner from the onset. Amazing, especially since the stumbling blocks that were placed before Royce the night before. He could've cancelled and that was understandable. It wasn't much fun hanging out in front of a store for nearly an hour and a half either, but we waited. He'll wake up sometime. But all this was only the LORD mapping out HIS strategy. Be patient and keep faith because everything is on HIS time. We couldn't have found that particular tree in the dark. Most of all, had we been in position before daylight, we would've climbed back down by 10:00, thus never seeing those deer coming out to feed nearly an hour later.

*Glen and Cory with a small deer.*

Thank you, GOD, for the angel you sent us through Royce. This trip meant a lot to a father and son who hadn't got to enjoy the outdoors together in a long time. Learn to cherish those moments with your children. They may move far away one day. It can be really tough, especially since they may have your only grandchild with them. "Leave him with us. We'll take care of him!" doesn't work.

I was invited to go on a hog hunt with Randolph Cox of Jesup, known to many as the "Public Land Prowler" on the *GON* Forum. I was eager to go, as this was an added acquisition to a fairly new WMA. It was really appealing since the floodwaters of the mighty Altamaha River had created a true island of hog hunting paradise totaling nearly a thousand acres. There was hardly any dry ground in the river floodplain for many miles, upstream and downstream, except for here. I videoed a segment of our boat ride through the flooded timber. When I completed filming, I noticed the film duration icon blinking on the digital screen. It said "1 min 11 secs." EEEW....I looked at PLP and said, "We're gonna get em!" Well, we got off to a rocky start, with each of us botching a couple of opportunities. In the end though, we both arrived back at the boat with a total of three hogs. PLP killed a large boar and myself, two of the plumpest gilts I'd ever seen. I could nearly taste the succulent meat melting in my mouth as I quartered them up.

*Glen with a black and white pig.*

Here's another memorable experience while hunting, and one of the best even though I didn't bag any game. In late December, I was bowhunting Lake Eufaula one evening and left my boat docked downhill from the cabin. The evening had been calm and the waters smooth as glass. I planned to go hunting the next morning, but when I awoke to a major temperature drop and gusty winds, I rolled back over. Mistake! Heading downhill to the dock at midmorning, I noticed white-caps on the lake and my bass boat nearly sunk! It was flush with the top of the water and beating against the dock. Thanks to SeaTow's services, it was saved from a total loss. Sadly, the estimate to repair and replace items lost or damaged, plus rewiring and practically rebuilding the motor, computerized components, etc. was several thousand dollars. OUCH! The next two weeks were spent in a constant state of worry wondering if my insurance carrier was going to cover my loss. There was no way I could afford to, and I hated to know I would still have to make payments for years on a fairly new boat that I'd never get to use again.

The day of their decision came while I was hunting a new WMA on the other side of the state, off the Altamaha River. There was a lot of pressure in the easier to access areas from the interior. Unfamiliar with the area, I studied the map finding the most distant section of land from the road along the river. I noticed the river made a very long bend creating a large peninsula of land at least a mile away. With the GPS, I lined up my compass bearings with those of the map from the road and made a projected waypoint one mile distant. I knew once in the swamp, the detouring myriad of sloughs and oxbow lakes would be too much of a Bermuda Triangle to run a straight shot. Great gadgets, these GPS's. Mark a spot you've never seen. After a few hours of weaving around countless sloughs of deep water, I could see daylight through the trees, exposing the wide run of the river. I was already at the one-mile point, not missing the river by much, just a little farther to go. I wanted to mark the tip of this peninsula for access from the river by boat on future hunts, especially with the multitude of hog sign. They're definitely working through here, just not today.

Tired, I nestled myself comfortably among the exposed roots of an ancient tree that rimmed the bank of the river. While resting and enjoying the sights and smells of the Altamaha, my cell phone vibrated...at 1:11. "Hello?" It was the insurance adjuster. After formalities he said, "We've talked with the boat repair facility and told them to proceed with the repairs. Your loss will be covered!" AMEN!! After a heartful talk with GOD, I prepared for the long walk back. With the GPS, I marked the exact spot where I rested and talked to GOD. Then I hit the marked waypoint for my truck. The distance shown was... 1.11 miles! Confirmation before and after! Think about this, if GOD is there before and after, it means that the betweens, those times you go through things, HE is there also! Should we always need proof? If 111's stop popping up and confirming things in my life today, I wouldn't be regretful. HIS signs have shown me irrefutably HE is always with me and for me! Maybe their purpose was to build my faith, seeing is believing. But now, I don't need to see to believe.

*"Then said Jesus unto him, Except ye see signs and wonders, ye will not believe"* (John 4:48, KJV).

NOW BACK TO 111 AT THE BEGINNING:

My friend David had come in from Florida to hunt a total of 10 days. Half the hunt would be across the lake in Alabama, hunting Barbour Co. WMA on a rifle hunt and bowhunting around Lake Eufaula, in both states. Woo-wee, little did he know he would center up that 10-day non-resident license perfectly with some of the coldest weather either of us had ever experienced, definitely for his little tangerine butt. Teens and low twenties the whole trip with wind chill factors in the single digits. He would remember his first Alabama trip for a long time. It was a tough hunt on an unfamiliar area. I passed three does the first day and missed one on day 3. I got an excuse, but you don't wanna hear it. Seen a couple more across a clear-cut, but it was way too windy for a shot that far. However, David was successful on one full day sit, killing a tailwind doe that blew by at 3:00 p.m. David impressed me with his endurance, especially from someone that wears insulated coveralls when it's 60 degrees. It was definitely an accomplishment of the days we hunted, with the daily temperature averaging 16 degrees and 30 mph wind gusts! His new nickname, the "Ice Man!"

Day 6 of the hunt - 1/11. That morning was even more brutal, so I decided to drive over to Fort Rucker to help David get his hunting permits and to register his weapons for a future hog hunt next spring and maybe even return a day to deer hunt. It would be worth a trip just to get all the formalities out of the way. I had discovered a lot of hog hunting opportunity here while researching an article for *GON* magazine and was anxious for a return trip there. We got back too late that afternoon to go to the Alabama side of the lake to bow hunt, so I opted to run a few miles away to the Pataula Creek tract of Lake WFG WMA.

I decided on a couple of new spots I'd pre-scouted late last season. I dropped David off near a line of rubs and scrapes on a pine hill next to an old beaver pond. I headed farther down the ridge, arriving at a small cluster of late-dropping water oaks that ended downhill at a swampy drain full of briars and vines. Last season this drain was full of buck sign and beds. Maybe I wouldn't get winded as the deer moved uphill to feed, if any were there.

About deer time, I sat there thinking, "I should be standing up now, in case one comes up behind me." I had my stand facing quartering away to keep from being too exposed because the only climbable tree was out in the open. Then, I heard a crunch in the leaves. You know where. Behind me. I looked slowly over my left shoulder. It was a doe in the wide open! Had I been standing and owl-turning my head constantly scanning the woods, I would be at full draw now. Another doe quickly joined her, and they began their descent up the ridge towards me. I could tell she was nervous, possibly catching a twinge of my scent in the swirling winds. The lead doe looked up at me once, but fortunately she didn't spook at the strange blob of growth latched on the side of the big pine. Maybe she could hear the chanting in my head, "Big squirrel, big big squirrel, only a squirrel!" She proceeded uphill until she was directly under me. The second doe moved up and took her turn ogling at the puffy camo'ed tree ornament. For at least three minutes we had a staring contest including the old head tricks, the drop and jerk upright method and the turn and whip back method, trying to tempt me to move. Man, deer all under me, can't even draw! The lead doe dropped her head to my stand's shoulder straps, which in my earlier haste, had forgotten to bury under the pine needles. When she got a good whiff, she jumped back a few feet, nearly sideways, turning broadside as a billboard. Just beautiful, errr... still sitting, bow in my lap. The other doe finally joined the first and they both started circling out of the opening into the adjacent cover. I'm watching two heads at once, waiting on a chance. The head of the second doe finally blurred behind a screen of oak shrubs. Now, one more periscope to go. The first doe turned and took off in a brisk walk to join the other into the same thicket. In less than a yard, she too would be shielded and out of my life. From my sitting position, all in one fluid motion I threw up my bow cocking its cams on the rise, shoulder crease in the peep...SNAP, THUNK! Had Quick Draw McGraw been there, he would've certainly said, "Dadgum!' She did a bronco kick and streaked towards a huge live oak forty yards away, dropping down out of sight behind it onto the descending ridge. The last few yards she was flagging, but that really doesn't tell you anything certain. On some deer, their brain just forgot to tell them they were dead. Sharp broadheads can cause that. On the flip side, a tucked tail isn't a guarantee either. I've even had deer run off and blow at me after a lethal hit. Always follow up! I waited a few minutes, got down and retrieved my arrow. Yeah! It was covered in blood. I seen a little grit. Gut or sand? Maybe I didn't hit one of them prickly limbs I had to shave-shoot by as the deer entered the thicket. Maybe just exited a little back. I thought, "Naw, this deer is definitely dead."

I figured I would find the deer a short distance behind the big oak. Wrong. After a few minutes I found the first drop of blood along a dim game path along the swampy drain downhill from the oak. I marked it and backed out, retrieved my climber and returned to the truck. Meeting David, we loaded our gear, grabbed some extra flashlight batteries, said a prayer and headed back. We had success finding a few drops here and there along the dim trail a hundred yards or so and then they just ended, completely. The deer seemed to be on a death run as it was a pretty straight line of travel with running tracks. I searched ahead on up the trail for a good distance with no results. We gridded off the area encompassing the last blood for a couple hundred yards square, hoping the deer curved off, crashing nearby. Nothing. We started at the blood again. This time, in an ever-widening circle. I finally found a few drops of what I thought was blood looping back in the direction of the swampy drain. Part of the drain was an old cutover that had grown up into a jungle of briars and vines intertwining among old treetops. Perfect place for a hit animal to head to for security. By the sporadic amount of "blood" I was now finding along with walking tracks, I decided to back out until morning. The tracks showed the deer was now meandering, meaning it was looking for a place to lie or to elude its trackers. Two hours of searching. The meat will be fine tomorrow as the temps would be in the twenties tonight. Don't wanna push her. No problem, she'll be nearby. Even though it was rough cover, the swampy drain was only a couple acres in size and the surrounding area of hardwoods was fairly open, surrounded somewhat by a field and the lake. It would be far easier to search in the daylight. The last blood I found, David was hesitant to agree with me that it was blood. He said it was something oozing and dripping out of some type of tree. Maybe that was the last blood on the straight-a-way. Before leaving, we looked an additional hundred yards beyond the last found blood drop, and....nothing. We had planned to return to Fort Rucker the next day for a one-day hunt before returning to Alabama. As I knew David would rather gun hunt, I told him I was sorry, but we would have to return here. I have an ethical responsibility as a hunter to exhaust all efforts.

*"The slothful man roasteth not that which he took in hunting: but the substance of a diligent man is precious"* (Proverbs 12:27, KJV).

That night as I stepped into the shower with a poked-out lip, I felt the Holy Spirit comfort me, with a feeling of calmness and warmth, a very different warmth than the hot water pelting my skin. I smiled, knowing then I would find my deer the next day. Before daylight, I put David up a tree on a hardwood ridge. I waited till dawn and crept to where I had climbed the evening before. I planned to sit on the ground for the first hour or so of daylight until the sun brightened up the woods. I would then begin my search for the doe, my primary objective.

Well, fast forward, I didn't find it that morning after nearly 4 hours of combing the tract. I circled the swampy drain, then crisscrossed and finished by gridding it off, searching every little thicket of cover. If there'd been a dead rabbit in there, I would've found it, even in the thickest of cover. Resting where I'd started, I heard a barely audible drop on the leaves besides me. Looking up, I expected to see a squirrel nipping tree buds. Nothing. Then I heard it again. Looking down quickly, I seen a small willow oak leaf quiver. I bent down and picked it up. Looked just like a blood spatter, but with a slight tinge of brown. Before leaving, I went on down toward the lake, 300 yards away, reading the wet sand and scanning the shallows. Disheartened, we returned to the cabin for a quick lunch that my wife, Cindy had prepared. I brought the last leaf back with me that I'd marked last night in the swamp. Cindy has excellent color vision. Soon as I opened my palm, she quickly said, "Not blood!"

Maybe that deer had stayed on a straight line of travel along the dim game trail. The only other sign I'd seen past the last blood was some pine needles kicked from a running deer 40 yards further ahead. Maybe it had broken a distant record for a death run. I was confident the deer was dead somewhere, since the blood appeared to be the color of heart blood and it did the bronco kick leaving out. I assumed the deer had veered off toward the thick drain or beyond it to the lake. There were fresh walking tracks leaving the trail heading downhill in that direction. But now, it appeared to be that of another deer. I would've walked even further out straight ahead had the terrain not gotten thicker. Anyway, we'd gridded off the area in the direction of the trail 200 yards.

Light bulb! "Cindy, you going with me!" She has proven herself before in a difficult tracking situation. I'm partial color-blind being weak in the green and reds spectrum. She's my helpmate, right?

"Sorry, David we're going back to Pataula again." I knew he was getting a little frustrated as his remaining days were dwindling, and he would much rather gun hunt on the Alabama side. He was probably thinking, "Man, when you gonna give up? Mutst've been a bad hit."

Another prayer and we were on our way. Thirty minutes later, Cindy was on her hands and knees searching intently ahead of the last marked droplet. I told her I was going to look ahead. Leaving, I swung wide, then came back in placing myself in a direct line of travel a hundred yards ahead and back onto the same dim path. That would give her plenty of room to work. I planned to ease straight ahead. A couple hundred yards later, the path played out. I stayed straight ahead, now with the terrain turning into a scrub oak flat. I noticed a disturbed oak leaf. Looking closely, I noticed a few grains of sand on it. Every few feet, another leaf the same way. Some kind of animal, big or small had been through. The ground was still frozen and other than the disturbed leaves, the rest was plastered flat to the ground. After crawling 60 yards, I finally made it to an opening. It was a rocky clay section of old woods road the forest hadn't reclaimed yet. No tracks or blood stood out. On the opposite side was a wall of wild plum bushes entangled with vines and privet. Had I not been on my knees I would've never noticed the small tunnel only 18 inches high from the ground in the dense foliage. I stooped down and immediately noticed a faint glimmer. A tiny speck of red. BLOOD! I hollered to Cindy and told her to come on ahead. I showed her my little prize. It was music to my ears when she said, "That's definitely blood!"

Behind the wall of cover I could see another 40 yards. Still no deer in sight. All this time, David was on the sidelines hanging behind Cindy. He was about walked out, searching in all other directions in case the deer had circled. He was also anxious to get on stand for the evening hunt. I told Cindy I would be back in a few minutes and carry on as I knew it was still going to be a slow track. I returned to the truck with David and motored him to a spot at the far end of the tract to undisturbed territory. It was only 60 yards from the highway and if you knew right where to look from the road you could see him. I'd observed deer here before crossing the paved road right before dusk, coming onto the WMA.

When I returned she'd found nothing more. That was the last of the blood. That's it! I said another short prayer, lined myself up with the deer's line of travel and took off. It was difficult to stay straight with all the low-hanging oak limbs and visibility only averaging 30 yards. After 250 yards of prickly limbs scratching the p-fire out of me, my enthusiasm had worn to a nub. Finally getting to stand up and straighten in a small opening, I noticed the woods appeared to open up and take on a different appearance. I walked a little further and came out on a mixed pine/hardwood ridge. Before me, a little less than a hundred yards away was a fairly open and deep valley of old mature hardwoods. Beyond that I could hear dogs and people, where a small community of people lived along the lake. "Well, might as well trot on up there and take a gander over the lip, done come this far." I stood there a moment gazing at GOD'S beautiful creation, amazed by the majestic and panoramic view of the towering giant white and red oaks. Turning to leave, I spotted something white out the corner of my eye. Probably another old bleach jug. Fifty yards away.... laid a DEER! I blinked my eyes, yep, still there! HALLELUJAH!! Never Give Up! I knew I was meant to find this deer! Even though 111 didn't play the roles I described earlier, I merely hoped I would be successful on that particular date just to have a sense of related significance, coming from my end, so to speak. Wow, 7 hours of total searching, traipsing over a hundred acres of woods and two return trips beyond the initial evening hunt. Miraculously, the deer had traveled over 500 yards. Later, I found out the arrow took out the onside lung and the heart going out. The temperature never reached 40 degrees that day. No bloating, smell, or green on the meat. Strangely, the deer was hardly stiff, and the cavity blood was still runny, not gelled and darkened. GOD had put it on ice for me, Amen!

Normally, under these circumstances I would've quartered the deer up where it lay. But being David had looked so long and hard himself, I decided he was going to lay eyes on this deer too. I owed him that. With me and the deer on the tailgate, we crept down the county paved road so David could see us go by. Knowing right where to look in the treetops, I held a thumbs-up as we neared. Making eye contact, I patted the deer on the side and seen his smile, big as mine flashing back through a small hole in the pine boughs. AIN'T GOD GOOD!

I don't regret the arduous task it took to find this deer one single bit. If I could rewind to yesterday evening and have the deer drop in its track, I wouldn't ask for a redo. Otherwise, I would've never gotten to feel such an overwhelming sense of accomplishment and elation. What a rush! All natural. After the fist pumps and the adrenaline dump wore off, I searched within myself, pondering what was the reason for this journey? A test of sorts? While later writing this, the reason hit me like a ton of bricks, might as well carved it on my forehead. IF I HAD THE SAME TENACITY IN MY WALK WITH CHRIST as I did for hunting and searching for a little ole doe, WHAT THINGS ARE POSSIBLE? A lot of us want to be better Christians and do more for the LORD but ask yourself, how hard are you trying? Are you giving it 110%? I mentioned Never Give Up earlier. What if we apply that same mentality to not cease from Praying daily? Praising HIM daily? Studying HIS WORD daily? Sharing HIS WORKS daily?

GOD has blessed my family and me beyond measure. HE has always been there for me, and ashamedly, I haven't. I challenge everyone to make a change in themselves. JESUS CHRIST laid out a blood trail for you. You know where it ends. You know what the gift is. YOUR SALVATION! JESUS CHRIST DIED FOR YOUR SINS SO YOU COULD HAVE AN EVERLASTING LIFE. HE PAID THE ULTIMATE SACRIFICE. HE'S not asking you to suffer through the same thing, but only to live your life as a Christian should, giving HIM Honor and Praise and telling others of HIS Works and Greatness. Ask HIM, what can I do for you? What is my gift and how can I use it for YOUR GLORY? There are numerous other holy duties. So, get off the bench, me included!

*"Now there are diversities of gifts, but the same Spirit. And there are differences of administrations, but the same LORD. And there are diversities of operations, but it is the same GOD which worketh in all. But the manifestation of the Spirit is given to every man to profit withal"* (I Corinthians 12:4-7, KJV).

Now, you have officially survived my ramblings. I tend to go WAAAY out when I write, so hang on for the ride and we'll pull back onto topic after a few thousand words. Maybe someone got a blessing or an answer from this story. Some may think, "Just some looney hollering about a lucky number, play Cash 3 with them!" Or a sarcastic hunter thinking, "Wow, such a riveting story about a little dinky doe, Whooppee!" It seems weird to me too, but in a divine way. I got a barn full of mounted trophies, antlers, and hundreds of photos from 30 years of chasing whitetails. I could tell endless and exciting tales about some of these animals, but I chose to talk about this seemingly insignificant doe. I believe GOD used 111 and the soul-stirring journey of this deer as the mechanism to enthuse and encourage me to finally write it all down. Or maybe to initiate something else. It may be a smaller part of a bigger PLAN that's still in development. I was very reluctant to write this, as some may want to run out looking for 111 or some other number. I don't want anyone to do that. Remember, Satan, the Great Deceiver has a proxy for everything. If you go to seeking for stuff on your own without HIS GUIDANCE, Satan will quickly divert your path in the wrong direction. It's not a lucky number, just a personal confirmation to me that GOD can be manifested in us. GOD, not chance, decides what happens in human affairs. Every decision is from the LORD.

*"The lot is cast into the lap: but the whole disposing thereof is of the LORD"* (Proverbs 16:33, KJV).

You need to pray and ask GOD to intervene and work in your life the way HE sees fit. Let him be your Everything in Everything! To my family, the confirmations of 111 is tangible evidence from GOD that HE has been keeping a daily presence in our lives, spiritually opening windows and doors for us at those exact and opportune times, directing our paths and rewarding our lives. Also, when you feel the HOLY GHOST during those interventions, you will definitely know it is of HIM!

*Glen with daughter, Candace, hunting on Ossabaw Island.*

## CHAPTER 1 EPILOGUE by Bill Prince

After Glen's death and before we had decided to publish Glen's writings, Corey, Glen's son, texted me asking if I was aware of his dad's belief that the number 111 and variations thereof were always proof to Glen that his thoughts, words and activities were confirmed by God as being God's will for Glen's life at that time. Since I was reading the manuscript of what is now this Chapter One of Glen's Book, of course, I knew about it and told Corey about the manuscript that I had. Corey said and I quote, "I got his death certificate this morning and his time of death was 11:01." I still have Corey's texts in my phone.

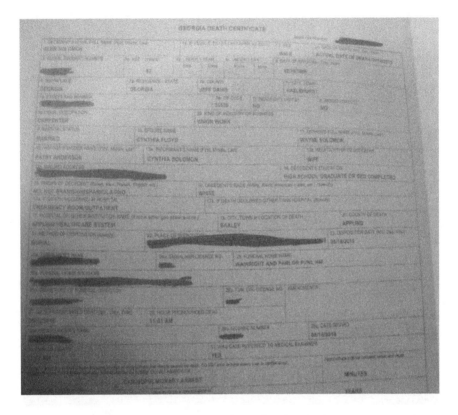

Bible believers know that God works in mysterious ways; many verses speak of this concept. I have chosen one verse to capture the thought that Glen was guided by God's confirmations.

*"For who hath known the mind of the Lord, that he may instruct him? But we have the mind of Christ"* (I Corinthians 2:16, KJV).

If the time of Glen's death doesn't show the continuation of God's hand being on Glen and Corey convincingly to you then consider that while taking Glen's death certificate to the union hall, Corey stopped to pick up some fishing tackle for which the amount was $11.11.

Corey later texted me again to show further confirmation from God. Here is a quote of Corey's text:

"When dad passed, we had two regular season and one club tournament left to fish. I decided that Dad and I were gonna finish the season together. I fished those last three solo with Dad as my partner in spirit. The tournament at Eufaula was our last regular season tournament and was also the one we looked forward to the most because of our cabin there. It turned out to be a very tough tournament and by far my worst finish on Eufaula. Although I caught several fish and lost a couple, only one fish measured to legal length. The weight of that one last fish was the cherry on top of mine and dad's last tournament season together."

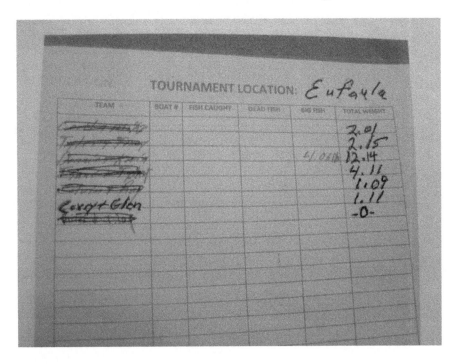

"The wind bloweth where it listeth, and thou hearest the sound thereof, but canst tell whence it cometh, and wither it goeth; so is everyone that is born of the spirit." (John 3:8, KJV)

Hunting on the Fly

# Chapter 2
## Etiquette and Tips for WMA Hunters

By Glen Solomon
Published by *GON*, September 4, 2018

**Do unto others... and you might find yourself rewarded with antlers.**

You've just settled in your stand. In a few moments the grayness of dawn will bring the woods to life. For a while, maybe since last season, you've been longing for this moment, this spot. Comfortably you await, and then you see it—a flashlight approaching. You flash back, but it comes nearer and nearer. Less than 50 yards away, whoever it is stops. Minutes later, you hear the sound of crunching bark as another hunter ascends a nearby tree. Enthusiasm and anticipation now become worry and frustration.

Does this sound familiar? Why or how did it happen? Is it their fault, or is it something you could've prevented? Can you adapt and still salvage your hunt? Can you learn from it? Lots of questions, with lots of answers.

Realize a WMA is public land. Some folks among the many may not be respectful or simply just not adept at maneuvering through the woods. I've even met some who were scared of the woods and only wanted to hunt near others, strangers or not.

Today, there are a lot of WMA newbies. From decades of experience, my WMA peers and I learned answers to many of these questions. Here are a few tips and suggestions to aid in WMA mutual harmony, success and enjoyment.

**1. If it looks good from the road, it will attract others:** Scout places people tend to drive by because it doesn't have "curb appeal." It may look too thick and nasty or have no climbable trees, steep terrain and no nearby pull-off spots to park. Many times a band of seemingly impenetrable cover may hide a very nice spot.

On Georgia WMAs, we have a lot of young pine plantations. Most folks tend to drive on by them. Get among them and find those odd scattered trees that are big enough to climb. Always keep a limb saw handy, as the limbs will be lower than the more mature trees.

If there are no climbable trees, always be open to the idea of hunting on the ground (OTG) with chair or blind. A tree is not required to kill a deer.

**2. Hunt overlooked spots right under people's noses:** Over the years, some of my best spots have been right behind or beside check stations, gun ranges, four-lane highways with its roaring traffic, narrow strands of cover, or the very first places you come to when you enter a WMA.

**3. Avoid spots with lots of ribbons, markers and foot trodden paths:** Especially avoid these areas when you see varying ages and colors of markers. These areas will guarantee unneeded drama at some point. Somebody will definitely come in on you, and there will be lingering residual scent. I like to find spots with no history of use, even snubbing those with one rusted glow tack or a tree that was once climbed long ago. I'm always searching for that hidden honey hole that will produce for years to come.

*Jonathan Bamford, of Tifton, says, "For the past five years I have had to go behind this guy and pull his flagging tape. Please, please, please, pull your flagging tape when you come out of the woods. I don't know about y'all, but I love our WMAs and see it as a privilege to have them. Therefore, I want to keep it clean and free of trash. I am a forester, so I understand the use of flagging tape to mark SMZ boundaries, plots etc., but flagging a trail and leaving it is unacceptable, and we must do better."*

**4. If you feel the need to use ribbon, mark the dates you will be hunting there:** If you feel the need to hang your climber early, it's a good idea to go ahead and run a ribbon trail and date your ribbons. When you are done with your hunt, please take all ribbons down. Do not place excess ribbon or place a ribbon across an entire access road or other opening.

If you see fresh ribbon, please be courteous and honor someone else's hunting spot if they beat you there. A good tact to take is first-come, first-serve.

**5. Do not hang your climber early or you may get blocked from your area:** Only hang a climber the day before if you are highly confident you are deep or hidden enough. If not, you will likely find yourself in a flashlight war that could end in hurt feelings. Most will be determined to get to their climber, like it or not. The other guy may not have scouted the day before and does not realize you even have a climber in the area. By the Golden Rule, he was there first. However, had I seen a dated ribbon, I would've gone elsewhere.

**6. Have a back-up spot should someone beat you to your first choice:** If you place an early climber, have a second climber in your truck should you have to relocate. Simply go to another pre-scouted choice. You could pull the other stand when the other folks leave at midday. Or they may move on after that one sit. Scout for nearby spots in the same block of woods. If you're on the stand and someone comes into your immediate area, simply slide down and move deeper or off to the side, perhaps across the drain or over the ridge. I have ditched the climber and went OTG nearby.

**7. Stay quiet when you make eye contact:** Whether someone comes in on top of you or is just going deeper in the woods, use sign language. Put your index finger to your lips. Everyone knows the universal sign for "Shhh." Give them a thumbs up, and motion them on by. If they are not going beyond, maybe they will be courteous and turn around. There is no need to echo a full-blown conversation throughout the woods, especially those still, quiet cool mornings. If not spotted, most times I let them go on by because most folks will not whisper.

Last season, I was at Oaky Woods WMA. I'd found where a buck had been bedded earlier in the season as evidenced by his old rub clusters, pills and matted bed. I've found that if it's good cover, many pressured bucks will return to these spots as they do remember a safe haven.

As I was about to head in the little tunnel I'd sheared in a wall of roadside briars, a truck came flying up. Slamming on the brakes, a feller jumps out in a fast walk and 15 feet away says in a loud voice, "Hey, where ya going, so we won't mess each other up?" I did a "Shhh," but I don't think it registered.

I walked close enough to whisper, pointed and said, "Straight in there about 200 yards."

Loudly again, "Oh, we are going to be on the other side of the road. My brother is going farther down. We are going to come back this afternoon and put a ladder stand in there!"

I swear I heard everything echo at least twice and probably half the WMA heard it, too. Then his brother got out of the truck and slammed his door so hard it knocked the dried clay out from underneath it. It was funny at the time. They didn't mean no harm. I wonder why they didn't just pull off to the other side where they were going in at. At least the buck still arrived later in the morning.

*Myles Montgomery on the Georgia Public Land Hunters Facebook page reported this sign on Allatoona WMA. It says, "If you are hunting on either side of road you will have company and we will not move! 4 hunters are hunting in here Nov. 5-Jan. 1 all year both sides of road." The author points out that access trails are used on WMAs to access deeper and larger portions of WMA. If you hunt an access trail, expect company.*

**8. Most WMA walk-in only access trails are designed so multiple hunters can reach larger and deeper portions:** Some areas just do not have adequate road systems, and access trails may be the only route to traverse the majority of a WMA. Some of these access trails can be hundreds of yards or even miles long. This is probably the most prominent area that people will walk upon or past you, especially if you are one that may only go in 50 to 100 yards. I see this a lot. So, expect company, be courteous and quiet, and let everyone get in place. Similar to access trails but wider and straighter are power, gas and cable lines.

Once at Bullard Creek WMA, I was 100 yards or so walking down a gas line with my climber on my back. A guy gets dropped off at the road and comes running all the way to me. Out of breath, he haggled out, "I got a ladder stand right ahead of you."

I said, "Fine, I'm cutting off the gas line and going into the pines. I won't be looking down the gas line and will be way out of sight."

He seemed relieved and climbed atop his perch as I went by. Not long after daylight, I shot a heavy buck. Knowing I needed to drag him to the gas line, I decided to be courteous and looped out through the woods to let him have some time and his long view undisturbed.

About 8 a.m., I was back at my truck and saw two does pop out on the gas line 150 yards away. The does were trailed by an even bigger 8-point than I had shot. I waited for the shot. And waited and waited. What in the world? He walked to the far side of the gas line to where I could see the upper portion of the stand. Nobody in it! I reckon he lost his confidence because of my nearby shot at daylight. By saying all this, keep your butt planted during deer time, especially the golden hour of 8 to 9 a.m.

**9. Learn to use a hand-held GPS or your smart phone:** Having GPS is a very valuable for hunting and trekking across our public lands. I opt for the hand-held GPS, as a smartphone may not have good service in areas. Get a model that has the electromagnetic compass, which is more accurate when you are immobile or in thick cover. My favorite model is the Garmin 64s. You will have no need for markers scattered throughout the woods. One drawback of flagging and markers is they are a magnet to attract nosy hunters who are interested in where you are hunting. The GPS will put you in the most direct walk to your stand or alter a route in case you have to swing around someone, come in from another road, or get you back to your vehicle quickly in the dark after following a meandering blood trail, etc.

**10. Avoid "dock talk" at the check station:** Outside your trusted hunting group, do not brag on good spots, the great number of deer you consistently see there, the bucks you pass up, etc. If so, be prepared to lose them soon. Some "friends" may even race you there the very next sit.

*Meet "Team No Drama!" Decades of experience hunting and camping on Georgia WMAs has taught this crew how to avoid drama and enjoy harmony while hunting all across the state. They often get up at 4 a.m. to get ahead of the crowds to avoid conflict. They are (from left) Ernesto Concepcion, George Gillette, Glen Solomon and Armando Morales.*

**11. Get up early:** This tip will mitigate most drama. When camping on WMAs, my circle of friends and I usually set our alarms for 4 a.m. to 4:30. We dress, have a little small talk and leave to our spots before most people even get up. Once I park at a pull-off spot, I may take a catnap for a few minutes if I don't have a long walk. Have all your gear in order beforehand, so when you see the first headlights, you can take off quickly.

In a closing summary, scout well, find places that are deep or overlooked. Access trails that are lengthy, know where they end and what you can access from them. Avoid places that look good from the road. Avoid places that

73

already have ribbons or signs of frequent use. Get up early, and be there first. If you feel the need to flag, do so modestly and retrieve them when hunt is over. On the entry ribbon put date(s) you will be there. Maybe even a short note such as "stand in place" or ".17 miles SE" or "end of access trail."

Use a GPS efficiently. Study maps and aerials. Have alternative stand routes. If you are physically healthy, carry your climber in and out each sit. You will always be in position to adapt and not have to possibly run a gauntlet of hunters to get to your stand, which messes everyone up. If it's too heavy, buy a lighter one. If you feel you are too slow and/or make a lot of noise putting it on the tree in the wee hours, practice in the off season. Or get one that works better for you.

Don't forget the option of OTG. Besides scouting and precision use of your gear, one of the strongest attributes to be a successful WMA hunter is having the mentality to adapt. Learn to be nomadic and not glued to one spot. Learn the other hunter's historic patterns of use for each respective WMA.

Hopefully these tips can help you while hunting on public land, share with your peers and any newbies you may meet. Good luck, play nice and God bless this deer season.

# Chapter 3
## Mudfish Mayhem in the Okefenokee Swamp

By Glen Solomon
Published by *GON* on July 29, 2019

**The hotter the better when it comes to catching the all-powerful bowfin.**

"I got one!"

Oh yeah, my favorite words to hear on the water. I wheeled around to see George's rod bent over double.

Seconds later, a dark fish rocketed out the water and did a 5-foot tailwalk across the top of the black glass.

I was hollering, "Reel, reel, reel! Keep him tight!" I coached loudly as I knew it was a bowfin (mudfish), and that toothy mouth can sling a set of treble hooks back to you. Moments later, George Gillette, of St. Mary's, proudly held up his first Okefenokee bowfin and his first-ever Dura-Spin lure catch.

Over the years, I've communicated with biologist and writer Bert Deener on his Okee fishing trips. It's very exhilarating to find someone who loves the Swamp as much as I, and we regularly share adventures. Bert created the Dura-Spin a few years ago and has since been slaying a lot of bowfin, jackfish and at times, large warmouth. Two summers ago, I started flinging Dura-Spins with good success, mainly at midday after a morning of fishing for what I consider the more delicious species.

*Matt Rouse*

I always wondered how many mudfish could be caught in a day when they were biting good, which ultimately led to the idea of a friendly competition.

Back in August 2017, a friend and I wore out the bowfin at midday after a morning of warmouth and catfishing. Nearly every cast for two hours we were getting hit!

Bert usually fishes the east side of the Swamp near Folkston at the Suwannee Canal Recreation Area, and my haunt has always been on the west side near Fargo at Stephen Foster State Park.

So... I challenged Bert to a 'Dura-Spin Duel.' Remind you, he created the Dura-Spin. Dummy me! My partner and I got spanked.

Our format for the day was to fish from 8 a.m. to 1 p.m. We'd be fishing to see who caught the most and who caught the single largest bowfin.

George and I scraped up 15 bowfin, and Bert with Matt had 67. So, glad he took it easy on us. He routinely catches 100 bowfin in a four-hour period. The timeline and results are below.

## Bowfin EAST vs. Bowfin WEST
### June 18
**Bert Deener and Matt Rouse**
8-9 a.m.: Two bowfin. First bowfin was caught at 8:54 a.m.
9-10 a.m.: 11 bowfin.
10-11 a.m.: 18 bowfin. Bert caught their two largest bowfin at 8.28 and 5.07 pounds.
11 a.m. – 12 p.m.: 22 bowfin.
12 to 1 p.m.: 14 bowfin.
Total: 67 bowfin.

Additional species: One jackfish, six warmouth and two Florida gar.

Bert reports, "Firetiger-chartreuse blade was the best color, jackfish-gold blade second, then at midday the jackfish-silver blade, and then there was a half-hour period that the crawfish-gold blade was awesome and caught 10 to one. Then that color shut down, and the first two were best again. We had just a couple fish on a black-chartreuse blade.

"Bowfin bite best as the sun gets up high, and at the point where you become uncomfortable with the heat, it really turns on. It will be an even stronger bite in August during the dog days of summer when practically nothing else bites. I can usually catch 100 fish in four hours. During a good bite, it takes longer to get the fish off than to get another bite. For bowfin, we just cast down the middle of the canal and keep it spinning just above the muck near the bottom.

"My usual way to take them off is to get hold of them with a lip-gripper, like a Boga-Grip, and then use a hook remover, the kind you squeeze and the metal insert squeezes back into the tube and grabs hold of the treble hook firmly. When it goes right, you don't have to touch the fish, just use the tools to keep your hands from their teeth."

## Glen Solomon and George Gillette

8-9 a.m.: Two bowfin.

9-10 a.m.: Two bowfin.

10-11 a.m.: Four bowfin.

11 a.m. – 12 p.m.: Three bowfin.

12-1 p.m.: Four bowfin. George caught our largest, a split-tail 6.6-pounder.

Total: 15 bowfin.

Additional species caught: one jackfish, two redfin pickerel, one flier, five yellow bullhead cats and 14 warmouth.

*Bowfin can quickly change what colors they prefer to hit. It's always a good idea to have a lot of variations with you when you head to the Swamp. These are some the different color combos you will find in the Dura-Spin.*

I caught the first couple of fish on a crawfish-gold blade. I picked up two more on a firetiger-gold blade, and that ended my bite as far as bowfin. George caught the remaining 11 bowfin on a lime-green firetiger-gold blade on a rod that I had set up for him. That was the only color scheme the bowfin would hit after the sun got up good, and the only one I had, too. On other colors, we had dozens of boils and swirls at them, but they wouldn't commit. Constantly all morning, mudfish would come partially out of the water, gulping air, feeding and teasing us. Too, the whole food chain seemed to be on fire with panfish flittering everywhere. George and I even caught three yellow bullheads and a flier trolling a Dura-Spin at 6 mph. Go figure.

The bowfin must have been keyed onto something very small. We tried 16 different colors and varying retrieves to no effect. Only the one lime-green version was effective.

Bert and Matt in the East win by a laaaandslide! Congrats guys! Until next year…

Then my Okee vacation continued.

After kicking off my annual Okefenokee trip with East vs. West, George and his wife Delia spent the remaining days with me in this regional paradise. Here we go:

**June 18 p.m.:** George, Delia and I had a relaxing evening fish fry, enjoying the tasty incidental catches of the morning's mudfish tournament. They said they were some of the most delicious fish they have ever eaten, even further amazed by the jackfish. I showed George how to prepare them by gashing, resulting in some big chunks of white flaky meat.

We concluded the evening with a scenic drive down the Sill and the Park Road, viewing the scenery and wildlife and videoing a lot of deer, turkey and gators. There is a certain aura down here. C'mon on down, and let it permeate your soul, does mine.

**June 19 a.m.:** George and I launched below the Sill into the Suwannee River. We fished for an hour and caught 26 warmouth, nothing big, just good eating size. Most were caught with the Magic Warmouth Worm, a 4-inch green-pumpkin plastic worm that I'll show you if you go over to www.gon.com/fishing/suwannee-river-warmouth.       Just scroll down to the bottom of that page, and I'll tell you what kind of worm it is and where you can buy it.

George threw a curly tail Beetle Spin. The river was very low and a little aggravating to get around, so I suggested we run back to camp and pick up Dee and fish the upper Sill before it got too hot. There, the water still flows out of the Narrows, which comes out of Billy's Lake that lies within the main Okefenokee Swamp. Good choice. Dee had a great time catching several yellow bullhead catfish and warmouth. George and I chose to fling Dura-Spins to see if the mudfish bite was better here. The lower Sill is always great, but by early summer, it gets too low and muddy. Here at the upper portion above the flood gates, the pure black water of the swamp is still trickling out to the river.

*Thanks to the author, George Gillette is now hooked on the excitement of fishing for hard-fighting bowfin.*

In the hour we were there, we caught 17 bowfin and a couple dozen or so warmouth. Surprisingly, the Dura-Spin caught two more catfish. Usually those are caught with bait or shrimp on the bottom, as Dee was using. I also caught three more redfin pike. I have never caught any of these here.

**June 19 p.m.:** Late afternoon we had another tasty fish fry under the shady live oaks. George and I went down the lane from Griffis Fish Camp to the landing on the Suwannee River, which is a few miles down from the Sill. It's a little deeper water here, once you get across a couple shallow areas. Dura-Spins kept us busy for a couple hours, racking up 11 jackfish with many more missing or slinging the hook. Those acrobatic little devils! Also, we caught 12 mudfish, and we lost count of the warmouth.

**June 20 a.m.:** George, Dee and I returned to Billy's Lake in the interior of the Okefenokee. George and Dee caught a couple dozen of the butter cats with small pieces of shrimp, while I toyed with the flier on a bream buster. I use a little fly called a Yellow Sally and a teeny balsa cork designed by Bert's Jigs and Things.

It's very fun and primarily for flier, but warmouth love 'em, too, which I caught several that morning.

About 10 a.m., we moved to a little honey hole spot along a strip of cypresses. I pulled out the Magic Warmouth Worm, and within 30 minutes, I caught 23 warmouth with the last five in the bag. Dee was still tossing bits of shrimp and caught nine more warmouth and six catfish. George picked up seven more warmouth with a Beetle Spin.

**June 20 p.m.:** George and I stopped by the Upper Sill for a few minutes while out doing another nature drive. George caught more than a dozen mudfish and four jackfish on the Dura-Spin. It was non-stop on the flier bream with the Yellow Sally fly. Nothing big but a lot of fun.

**June 21:** I'm no idiot, so guess where I went on the last day before returning home? Only a few minutes swing out of the way, Suwannee Canal Recreation Area on the east side. I can't let Bert have all the fun! The west side will be on fire later for a trip in August, but for now, here I come Folkston! Sadly, George had to head home.

Awesome day! A 100-fish day!

Hunting on the Fly

# Chapter 4
## Walking Miles To Find Chickasawhatchee WMA Hogs

### MISSING MY FRIEND GLEN SOLOMON
Chapter 4 Introduction by Brad Gill
Published by *GON* on August 23, 2019

I still can't believe my friend Glen Solomon has gone to be with Jesus at the age of just 52.

I first met Glen on Saturday, Nov. 26, 2005 as I rolled into a campground on Chickasawhatchee WMA. We had coordinated a trip together so he could show me a thing or 10 about how to hunt public-land hogs. Little did I know I was fixing to get a crash course not only in hunting hogs but also in woodsmanship.

According to Glen's GPS, we covered 10 miles in 2 1/2 days, but Glen's never-quit attitude, and a hunting passion and a drive that I believe is unmatched, led to a pair of hogs, one of which was my first one from Chickasawhatchee.

"A day in the woods is never wasted," he told me. "If nothing else, you can eliminate ground."

I've been with *GON* since 1998, and I can honestly say that Glen is the man I'd rank as the No. 1 WMA deer and hog hunter I've ever known. That's naturally why he was such a good fit to become a writer. This guy stayed in the woods all the time. If he wasn't working, at church or with his family, then he was hunting or fishing. Ask anybody, they'll tell you the same.

Just before Glen passed, I pitched an idea for him to become a *GON* online blogger. He was so knowledgeable and well-liked that we felt like his blog page was worthy of selling its own advertising space. From my understanding, Glen had several companies already committed to buying the space.

I don't say this lightly, but Glen was a great writer who had a very special writing "voice," one that some full-time professional writers don't possess.

My opinion is that a writing voice is a God given talent, not something that can be taught. I joked with Glen that we were fixing to make him a rock star, but the truth is that he already was one in the eyes of so many who respected his woodsmanship and knowledge of Georgia hunting and fishing.

*GON Editor Brad Gill (left) with a Chickasawhatchee WMA hog from 2005. The hog was well-earned and came with a serious education on hunting hogs and woodsmanship from Glen Solomon.*

One character trait I learned very quickly about Glen was his very deep passion for Georgia hunting and fishing. His roots run deeper than any I know. Many of you reading this think you're passionate about your hook-and-bullet sports. Heck, I think I am passionate about them, too, but I really believe Glen was on a whole different level. He told me recently, "It's not a sport to me, it's a way of life."

Something else that made Glen even more special as a person was that while he's the best WMA prowler I ever met, he never let on that he thought so.

We recorded a podcast in July, and he said, "I try to tell people I'm not a know it all. I just love to talk about it. If you get me talking about it, I ain't gonna shut up. I just love it so much."

Glen loved these two sports so much that he wanted others to enjoy it at the same level, too. He wasn't shy about his "honey holes" and "sweet spots." Go to www.gon.com/fishing/blackwater-redbelly-slam, and you'll see what I mean. He listed 10 of his personal spots for *GON* readers to go and catch redbreasts. What does he gain from that? A giant blessing from sharing something he is so passionate about with others so they can go and enjoy it, too. I think many sportsmen miss that point in life. Not Glen.

Most importantly above anything printed above, Glen and I talked about Jesus a number of times over the last 14 years. Glen knows Jesus, he told me about the relationship that he had with Him. Glen didn't worship the creation, but he did worship the Creator. There is a difference.

Enjoy yourself at the foot of Jesus, and I'll see you soon my good friend.

Y'all please keep praying for the family, especially his sweet wife Cindy, and their son Corey and daughter Candace.

## WALKING MILES TO FIND CHICKASAWHATCHEE WMA HOGS
By Brad Gill
Published by *GON* on April 27th, 2006

When I first saw the black hog trotting between the palmettos, it was only about 30 yards away, heading right for me.

Best I could figure, I'd put about 10 miles under my boots in the last two days to get myself in this position. Just because hogs can't see or hear very well doesn't mean hunting them on a pressured WMA was going to be a cake walk. It wasn't, but it made that moment when I first saw the hog so, so rewarding. We'd done it, covered ground, found hogs and here was my big chance to actually kill one with a .22 magnum rimfire rifle — on Chickasawhatchee WMA!

My adventure to this southwest Georgia WMA began on the Saturday after Thanksgiving. I met Glen Solomon of Hazlehurst, his son, Corey, 19, and Don Wood from Waynesville at the western Chickasawhatchee WMA campground for what would be 2 1/2 hard days of hog hunting. The WMA was open to small-game hunting, which meant we could shoot hogs with small-game weapons. I was the only one who opted for a scoped .22 magnum rifle. My three hog-hunting buddies would hunt with muzzleloaders. Chickasawhatchee WMA is about 15 miles west of Albany in Dougherty, Baker and Calhoun counties. It's 19,700 acres of beautiful bottomland hardwoods and upland pines. Glen was the only one in our party who'd ever hunted Chickasawhatchee, but even his experience was limited. Glen's favorite WMAs are in southeast Georgia.

Last hunting season Glen and Don killed about 25 WMA hogs between the two of them, and they shot most of them with small-game weapons in August and February. These boys would quickly teach me something about how to find WMA hogs.

"We may have to cover a lot of ground before we find them," said Glen.

I had no idea exactly how much ground he was talking about. Glen and I headed for a section of mature pines above the Spring Creek drainage. Last year Glen said the area was covered in rootings, but after a fast-paced, 45-minute stroll revealing no sign we checked the area off our list.

"A day in the woods is never wasted," said Glen. "If nothing else you can eliminate ground."

Glen's WMA hog-hunting strategy is to walk and not stop until he finds a lot of very fresh hog rootings. Glen likes to see at least several acres of rooting that's less than 24-hours old. Since hogs can move miles overnight, Glen said that hunting two- or three-day-old hog sign is often worthless.

He often finds the freshest hog sign several miles from a road, where hunter traffic is low. Glen always carries a GPS, and he often wears waders to get him into places most folks won't travel.

From the pine stand we headed down into the Spring Creek drainage where we found a little bit of fresh rooting. Glen told me to go down the creek, and he would make a big circle and meet me. Fifteen minutes later I'd gone about 100 yards, and Glen was coming to me.

"No good… boot tracks all down that other side," said Glen.

Glen guessed the boot tracks were a week old, and the fresh sign we originally found was hogs starting to settle down and come back into the area. However, his quick stroll down the creek didn't uncover any fresher rooting. It wasn't enough sign to peak his interest.

That afternoon we covered about four miles on the north end along the Kiokee Creek drainage. We paralleled the open bottom inside a thick palmetto flat. We did find some fresh rooting and tracks. However, it was scattered and small, which told Glen it was probably just one or two hogs passing through. We checked the north Kiokee Creek area off our list.

The next morning the four of us headed a mile or so down Kiokee Creek, and we spent time weaving from creek bottom to pines, still looking for fresh rooting. Again, we found only scattered sign, so there was no reason to slow down.

For the afternoon, Glen and I split up in the powerline area of Chickasawhatchee Creek. I stumbled upon some fresh sign a little over a mile from the powerline, but again it wasn't much. Glen jumped a big hog out of a palmetto bush. "He was probably the only hog in there — I didn't find any sign," said Glen.

Sore-footed, we were wondering if we'd even find a group of hogs. It was nearing dark on day two, and we were in the truck headed to check one last place before dark. While driving we noticed rooting by the road. Glen told me to stop. He got out and looked at it. Surely, we wouldn't get lucky and find hot sign right by the road, would we? "Pretty old," he said.

About 200 yards later the sign seemed to take on a different, fresher appearance. With a half hour left before dark, we split up.

Jackpot! Both of us discovered several acres of fresh rooting on both sides of the roads, several hundred yards back in the woods. We got lucky on this one. Nobody had discovered the sign, or at least nobody was hunting these hogs. I guess most folks were still busy deer hunting on their clubs.

"In the morning we'll need to park way up the road and walk in," said Glen. "We don't want to bump them driving through here. A lot of people make the mistake of pulling right up to an area that has fresh hog sign."

Twenty minutes after daylight I was 300-yards deep and looking at a Chickasawhatchee hog wasting no time coming up the same small trail I was standing in. I shouldered my rifle just as the hog jutted off the path and paused briefly behind a palmetto.

In my head I kept hearing what Glen had told me the previous day, that .22 magnum is a mean gun. I'll shoot a hog in the shoulder with it, unless it's a big one.

What's a big one?

This black porker looked big enough that I knew I didn't want him to turn and run at me after being hit behind the shoulder with a small bullet.

The hog turned broadside and looked like he was fixing to walk back into the trail. I couldn't believe it... it was the moment we'd worked for.

When its head hit the clearing, I aimed right below the ear and pulled the trigger. I'd just taken the hardest-earned animal I'd ever worked for. We guessed the boar to be about 90 pounds, not what Glen classifies as a "big one," but he did put the boar in the "good-eating-size" category.

The four of us gathered back up for picture-taking and high-fives. I loaded my hog in the truck and went to quarter him up, while the other three continued to hunt. An hour later my cell phone rang.

"I just killed one, looks like a twin to yours," Glen said.

What an awesome hunt! Two dead hogs after really working for them. It's a neat feeling to walk your back-end off and then get treated in the end with success. To me, it's hunting at its best.

Chickasawhatchee WMA allows small-game hunting, which means you can kill hogs with small-game weapons, from December 29-February 28. Directions from Albany are in the hunting-regulation booklet.

However, don't limit yourself to Chickasawhatchee. Glen's tactics will work on any WMA that has hogs. However, if you're new to a WMA don't expect success right off the bat. We sure had to work for success.

Camp a few days, and just enjoy walking miles and miles in the beautiful swamp bottoms and pine hills of southwest Georgia. You may stumble into some hot sign, a hog or two and be rewarded with some of the best-tasting meat in the woods.

*Glen and Bill Prince eating BBQ after their last fishing trip.*

*Glen's last hog.*

*Glen with a big 10.*

*Glen uphill with hands raised, event unknown.*

*Glen with a wild turkey.*

*Glen with his biggest boar.*

*Jeffery & Candace (Glen's Daughter) with first deer taken together after marriage.*

*Glen and Ms. Cindy with her mother, Marilyn Floyd, at Candace's Wedding.*

Hunting on the Fly

# Chapter 5
## My Outdoor Hero

By Glen Solomon
Published by *GON* on June 8, 2016

Who is your outdoor hero? Many years ago, I was asked this question. I never did answer, but the faces of many flashed through my mind.

My Uncle James opened many doors of outdoor pursuits for me, such as my first trips for bedding bluegill, watching rabbits and beagles, looking for river-bottom squirrels and most important of all, fishing in the Okefenokee Swamp.

Perhaps hometown legends, such as Bird Dog Walker, who always bagged his game and loaded the boat, are your hometown heroes. Maybe old-school professional outdoorsmen like Chuck Adams, Knight & Hale, Bill Dance, Rick Clunn and Georgia's own Michael Waddell, are your heroes.

My personal hero is my son, Corey. He pursues game and fish for me while I am away on work travel, succeeding on many adventures afield and on the water. Through his eyes I live, so to speak.

Outside of family, I still ask myself who would be my outdoor hero that represented the many hunting circles I've been part of, who had a hand in the crossing of paths with endless other hunters. I've covered a lot of ground in this state, hunting more than 4-dozen of its public lands, been a member of several large clubs and been a lessee, as well.

There's also all the "sit a spell" hang-outs for those respective areas. In those spit-and-whittle spots, talk was mostly of hunting and fishing, not politics and smartphone games. Lots of hunting memories were exchanged. Memories are all we really leave behind in this world. They say memories are not tangible things, like a boat or a gun, but they are real things that come from the heart.

The primary reason I started outdoor writing was to store memories for my family to read in the future. I soon discovered another cause. Hopefully my writings create some excitement and enthusiasm for Georgia's outdoors. We all need to somehow play a part in promoting our outdoor heritage.

In saying all this, I know a someone who has made a huge impact for our hunting heritage, stretching over a period of 30 years right here in Georgia. Assuredly, this person was the catalyst for creating thousands of positive individual hunting memories. All this took place from a large hunting camp which surrounded a little field in Wilkinson County. The landowner and the person whom I consider to be my hero is Mrs. Jean Butler. If there was an equivalent of a Nobel Peace Prize for Georgia hunting, she should be a nominee.

To explain why Mrs. Jean was the catalyst for endless memories, consider these variables: During the 80s and 90s (the heyday hunting years), Mrs. Jean managed more than 80 different small- to medium-sized hunting club entities. Each club would average a lease or two with many having as high as six separate leases. Some leases had a clubhouse built on site, or they would have campers. However, most of these club members stayed at her camp in that little field in Wilkinson County.

Most leases would range from more than 100 acres upward to 1,200 acres or more. That's a lot of land and a lot of folks. I spent most of four seasons hunting there and actually lived there nearly two years. So, I had more good times than I can remember. On a busy weekend I have seen more than 200 people there, especially during events such as opening weekend, Thanksgiving and Mrs. Jean's camp birthday party.

Mrs. Jean rarely ever had to fix supper on the weekends, as there was always someone inviting her down for a cookout. This had to be one of the most thriving hunting camps in the entire United States. I will never forget the camaraderie, friendships made, kids playing, hunters telling tales, laughing, snoring, crackling campfires and taste buds always watering from the delicious smells that wafted endlessly around camp from the dozens of grills and cookers.

Back then gas was cheap and folks came nearly every weekend of deer and turkey seasons. This was also the era game cameras and timed feeders really took off, which made even more trips during the off season. Add trips for hogs, food plots, feeders, camera checking, etc. Wow! Lots of memories and tales culminated during those trips for sure.

Not only did Mrs. Jean operate the hunting camp (for the miniscule amount of $85/year, including water during the time frame I was there), she was the leasing liaison for practically all of Wilkinson County. That included land from private landowners and timber companies. If someone needed money for land taxes and their land was conducive for hunting, Mrs. Jean was the woman to see. Her reputation along with her paying up front for many of the leases ensured she had first dibs.

I call her a liaison, and not an agent, because I know not of her profiting from huge bonuses or markups as some agents or lease-flippers will do. If she did, it was merely rounding numbers. At times, she paid for some leases that hunters didn't renew for whatever reason. Those were the ones she would let me lease or hunt for free.

My little cabin was by the road going down to the main camp at the field. Everyone had to pass me. A few views at the cleaning rack and some of those leases would be back in demand. Anyhow, I like to remain nomadic.

"Gimme another one Mrs. Jean," I'd tell her. It always led to a little guiding or proper set-up pointers for the new members when I released one. Helping her with lessees by showing land and guiding and occasional help on the farm, she in return supplied us with some good groceries, garden vegetables and farm-raised pork.

I learned how to heat a syrup kettle, add a little lime and scrape a hog. I also learned how to butcher it and not hardly throw anything away. Mrs. Jean was sure quick with that butcher knife. We'd use the hog lard for cooking redbreasts from the nearby creek and taters from the garden. Also, she taught my son good work ethics at a young age by stretching miles of fence. Just recently, Corey said, "She was the only person I ever really enjoyed working with, never got mad at you or said anything bad. Always made you feel good. She was the same at the dinner table as she was working. I will always remember her laugh."

If you wanted land to hunt in Wilkinson County, you would call Mrs. Jean and tell her what you were looking for. When she found it, she made sure you had a nice campsite, even if she had to clear more woods near the field. I'll never forget the time that Mrs. Jean, in her 60s by then, and I were making a clearing for some new campers, and she took a chainsaw from me and showed me how to really use it.

Then there was the time she was digging more fence-post holes than I was in some hard, rocky ground. Every time she would go down with those post-hole diggers, sparks would fly. I figured she would give up before I did. Wrong!

Being a widow for many years, she learned to work harder than most. Her main source of income was from being the Water Department Superintendent in Irwinton and a school bus driver for Wilkinson County. Along with her daughter, Bonnie, Mrs. Jean also had the shared weight of tending the farm that was full of all kinds of livestock and fowl. Schools would bus their students out for tours. She had crop fields to plant and hay to gather, and there was always some kind of tractor work going on.

For a little side money on the weekends and holidays, she put up fence and gates for the county and also individuals. For a little pocket money and at times just enough for the tractor gas, she put in food plots for her hunters. She left it up to you what was in your heart or could afford to pay. Seems to me she was more into making friends than money.

Real cold weather would mean water pipes bursting. Being a water superintendent in a small town, she actually did most of the repairs. She would have an assistant at times, but after three or four sleepless nights in a row in below freezing weather, they didn't last long. While heading out to hunt in the early morning hours, I've seen her many times arriving home from standing all night in icy water fixing pipes. I can still remember her standing there constantly rubbing her hands to warm them up. I said, "You gonna go lay down, I know you're wore out?" She replied, "I got to hurry and clean up, get on the school bus, and then I got some more pipes to fix." Mrs. Jean was one tough lady!

Once, when she trained coon dogs for folks, she got lost at night in bad weather, and for cover, she slept in a culvert with the dog for warmth. She was amazing, as I have never had an elderly woman throw a tree climber on her back, walk with me a half mile back in the woods and shimmy up a pine 40 feet high just as fast as me.

Mrs. Jean was one of the toughest working folks I have ever met in my life. I do not know of two people combined who would've covered the ground she did in a day's time. Also, I can't fail to mention she had one of the most tender hearts I've ever seen. For example, at any time, if a hunter decided he didn't like his lease, or if she overheard one merely make a grumble about not having success, she would be quick to offer them a full refund of their money or get them another lease. Back then, it would be their fault, not hers, that they couldn't see or kill deer, as Wilkinson was really loaded with game back then.

If I was familiar with the tract, she would enlist me to help them succeed by actually guiding them to the stand or giving pointers. She treated everyone at camp like family and would strive to make sure they stayed happy.

There're so many memories of good times, laughs and smiles, and now, sadness and tears. I wish all the readers could meet her. Sadly, they can't. With great remorse, I hate to tell everyone that Mrs. Jean recently passed away. I didn't mention it at the onset because I wanted to share good memories rather than someone thinking they were reading just another prepared eulogy. Anyway, no one could ever write a eulogy well enough to appropriate her status as an icon in Georgia's hunting heritage.

Before her passing, one of the largest kaolin deposits in Wilkinson County had been discovered in and around camp. Mineral rights resulted in the hunting camp closing last year. With the passing of Mrs. Jean this past January and the closing of possibly the largest of Georgia's hunting camps in history, indeed marks the end of an era in middle Georgia. I am so glad God allowed me to see her one last time when I visited from squirrel hunting at nearby Beaverdam WMA. I was again interested in a possible lease there. Not now, it won't be the same. There's more to hunting than chasing game. Importantly, I still have my memories to cherish.

In closing, I, too, remember her laugh. To leave her family and mine a little humor in a dark time: Remember when the cow got stuck in the big mud hole below Jenna's house? All of us were either pushing or pulling with a rope to no avail. Mrs. Jean went and got the tractor to apply tension. When we had the old cow's neck stretched to the point of breaking, Mrs. Jean's muddy boot slipped off the clutch, the tractor lurched forward popping the cow out like the cork out of a wine bottle. I never knew that a cow's neck could stretch that far. She panicked a little and again patted hard for the clutch and brakes, but her muddy boots kept slipping off, looking as if she was stomping out a fire. By the time she stopped, she'd dragged the cow out in the pasture several yards. The cow lived, but it broke Mrs. Jean's heart at the time. Later, when we would share that tale with others describing that ol' cow's neck, she, too, would laugh with us. I can hear her now.

God bless her family and many friends.
RIP Mrs. Jean Butler,
Oct. 3, 1937-Jan. 7, 2016.

# Chapter 6
## On the Road with Glen Solomon

By Glen Solomon
Published by *GON* on November 1, 2008

Join the author on a month-long hunting trip across the state. He's hunting public land, searching for rut-crazed bucks.

My name is Glen Solomon. I am an addict. My addiction is hunting and the rush. I practice my habit on public land. The state of Georgia has many programs in which to help people with their addictions. The one I am a part of is the wildlife-management-area system. I've been hunting Georgia's public lands for 26 years. I hunt 'em for the challenge and variety, meeting new people, rekindling old friendships, learning new things and always having somewhere new to go.

For the first time, I will be keeping a diary of my hunts, along with tips, tactics and thoughts, just to show those people pouting and crying about nowhere to hunt just how much excitement and success can be had by joining the state's $19 hunting club. Seems like I keep reading in *GON* about folks quitting hunting because they lost their lease or hunting club. For some, that's the only place they have ever hunted. Listen up, there are more than a million acres in Georgia for you to find greener pastures and hidden honey holes, not to mention new memory-making adventures with your friends and family. Also, what about your children and grandchildren that you have taken under your wing or the ones you have yet to introduce to the great outdoors? Don't punish 'em. Carry 'em, and unfold new mysteries together while keeping our hunting heritage alive.

Ignore the horror stories about getting shot or stampeded by hordes of hunters. The only accidents I've ever read about in more than 20 years of reading *GON* happened on private land. If it's going on out there, they know. Plus, I have years of experience on more than three-dozen WMAs. On public lands, hunters are aware they may see another hunter at any time and will take time to identify their targets before raising a weapon. Do your scouting efficiently, and you will avoid the majority of other "orange" encounters.

Anyhow, I like crowded hunts. It makes the deer move, making my stands in escape funnels and trails in security cover more productive. Sometimes it is quite lonely on many of the sign-in hunts I attend. I used to be a club member and also leased my own tracts of land, but I have moved on to better things since. No more worrying about planting food plots, keeping feeders full and expensive crowded leases that you may or may not have next year. All time and investments are non-returnable and lost. For the cheap fee of $19, WMAs also provide biologists to boot. There is actually less pressure on most WMAs — as most are only open a few days a season — whereas most hunting clubs are pounded and stomped out year-round with a variety of activities. High hunter density lowers deer density. The surviving deer have everyone patterned.

For example, I hunt one WMA that runs for miles alongside several hunting clubs, separated only by a dirt road. To determine hot spots, I look for the coming and going of deer tracks in the road. The crossings will be very recognizable and churned up. Deer will typically work a circular or elliptical pattern. The trail going into the hunting club will be mostly night traffic raiding the food plots of the hunting club. The trail returning to the WMA will be headed to bedding areas; some will be near the road and others a mile or more away.

In evenings I hunt close to the road for staging deer and get a little deeper for morning hunts. One turkey season I walked near a road edge for nearly a mile. The terrain consisted of tall grasses, briars and small pines. I counted dozens of beds, some within sight of the road. Waiting on dark to play, huh? These deer know exactly what the sound of a rattling gate chain means.

Now, where was I? Oh yeah. On WMA check-in hunts, you are allowed two bonus tags, which is beneficial when you live off the land like my family. Stop eating meat from the grocery store. Consume only wild game, and in a few weeks or even days you will notice a drastic change in how you feel metabolically and mentally. It will ultimately lead to an abundance of energy you didn't know you had. Occasionally I run out of wild game and have to supplement from a grocery store. After a couple of days, the difference in how I feel is like night and day. Think about this, there are only four main meat groups uptown — beef, pork, chicken and fish. Deer is my "beef" ingredient for all dishes — it's fine right by itself. Wild hog sure has a pretty pink color. I catch my own fish. Turkey, dove and quail sure knock out chicken. Throw in a few squirrels and rabbits to complete a hunter's smorgasbord. Okay, drifting off the subject again.

So, don't be hesitant. Grab a tent, relax and stay the whole hunt. Enjoy camping. You remember that, don't you? Have fellowship with your family, friends and hunting peers. To me, it's kind of like stepping back in a lost or forgotten time, maybe "The good ol' days." Step out in the wild for a few nights. You will sense the soul-stirring I'm talking about, or maybe even conjure up some old memories.

Study the WMA listings in the hunting-regulation book, get a calendar and plan some hunts. You don't even need whole days, maybe a morning or evening out to the areas close to home. Georgia has a four-month season, so there will be several places open even if you have a tight schedule.

While I'm hunting on the fly, if our paths cross, holler at me. If I can help, just ask. My buddy, Garmin, always has some extra coordinates we can't cover. See you at the cleaning rack!

Here goes. Forgive me of improper sentence structuring and other grammar no-nos. This is my diary, and I'm writing it in a direct tone to my friends who share the life of hunting, not to literary scholars. Okay, I admit it, I'm a Redneck, and this is my story.

Nov. 1: Hannahatchee WMA

Hannahatchee is one of the most challenging WMAs in Georgia, where any legal deer is a trophy. It is overhunted due to a lengthy season and scarcity of public land in this part of the state. There's only three deer on the kill sheet since opening of firearms season.

I did some in-season speed scouting, checking on old waypoints. Nothing exciting found, just minimal scattered sign with no noticeable patterns. No deer seen or heard.

Even though there is a fair population of deer here, I have learned a lot of these professional eluders (deer) are looping back to bed on private property. The places I checked were in traditional-type areas such as drainages or along beautiful hardwood ridges. Sure, I saw a few scrapes and tracks here and there, and a place or two I might could kill a deer, but not "The Place."

My gut instinct told me if I was going to connect on these survivors (deer), I was going to have to "hunt ugly." Here, that means steep canyons of kudzu and briars. There are a few big pines in there, but you're going to need a machete to get to one. Start super early, since you need to chop on the morning you hunt — it's got to be a surprise.

There are also a few scattered deer hanging around short-pocket flats and ridges of low thick underbrush and scraggly scratchy pin oaks near the road right under people's noses. Find these spots adjacent to plots, roads, fields and right-of-ways. Hint — look for tracks in the roads and openings where they danced all night long, only to dart back in when they heard tires crunching gravel.

If you can walk in upright and unscathed or find a tree big enough to climb, you are definitely in the wrong place. Leave the clangy stand in the truck, crawl in well before daylight and sit on the ground where visibility is best — throw 'em a curve ball. For now, I have better and favorite hunts to attend.

A word of advice: Study the harvest data in the WMA Special in the August issue of *GON*, and play the percentages. I keep a copy in my map book at all times. Also, notice there are high and low cycles for some areas, which means hunts can actually be predictable.

I will be back here in December, if I have any tags left, after the foliage has fallen and hunting pressure has decreased. These deer here rut late.

Nov. 5: Lake Eufaula Public Land

P.M. Hunt:

Bow hunted OTG (on the ground) on a large water-oak flat that was raining acorns — thump, thump; it was like walking on marbles.

Three does followed by a 6-pointer and spike came in to feed. After 1 1/2 hours of watching them vacuum acorns, I had stalked within 60 yards. My Leafy Suit is awesome. Swing your bow arm back, putting your bow behind and perpendicular to your leg. Take baby steps, barely raising your feet above the leaves. Use the old Indian method of walking straight, not deviating left or right, and don't swing your appendages. I actually had a leaf balanced on my shoulder the whole stalk. No spider webs attached.

With my mouth, I grunted in the 6-pointer and spike to within 40 yards. Passed. Too early in the game.

Nov. 6: Lake Eufaula Public Land

A.M. Hunt:

Bowhunting. I climbed in the same oak flat. I was in the tree two hours before daylight. Deer were bedding on the open oak flat. I had to beat 'em there.

If I did bump them going in that early, I wouldn't be over-concerned. I have learned deer don't spook nearly as bad at night as they do at predawn or daylight. In the old years, I'd walk around in the dark with a climber on my back until I heard deer crashing off and then climb right there. More times than not, at dawn or a couple of hours thereafter, he, she or they would come slipping back in.

I think a deer will regard danger in one of two ways. Hey, I have a good place to escape again if danger approaches, or I better not get caught here again — I'm finding somewhere else.

By being super early, it gives them time to calm down, especially if they only heard you and didn't smell you. Plus, those deer were there for a reason, maybe a hot food source, and others will come. Also, bucks know where doe units frequent and may come by for a scent check later on. Okay, rambling again.

A few minutes after daylight, about 80 yards out, I observed four does feeding along, and all the while they were being harassed by a shooter 8-pointer. He was working them like a cutting horse, trying to nudge in for a scent check. With the new moon and cool mornings, I was witnessing some pre-rut activity.

After 45 minutes of watching frolicking deer in their playground, I determined they weren't coming any closer, so I pulled out my Knight & Hale rattle bag. First, I belched out two different tones of grunts, one with a cupped hand facing away to create an illusion of two different bucks meeting.

I hit the rattle bag, clashing and grinding for about 20 seconds. During the process, I threw in a few blows, snorts and some heaving-type grunts. Now a hundred yards out, the buck threw his attention to me. Hair bristling along his back and headgear cocked, here he comes! He was coming in like he was on a string. Then 40 yards out, he started to circle my position to get downwind. He hung up near my entry trail less than 30 yards out but was screened out by thick brush. It didn't take him long to get suspicious with no fight in sight. He then wheeled around and started trotting back to the does.

I gave a loud bleat with my mouth and immediately drew him back. He stopped in range, but dadgum, he was one small step too far forward. There was a tree lined up perfectly where my X mark was, tight behind the shoulder. I still had some lung zone exposed, but I would have to send my arrow right next to that tree on an alert deer. If that tree bark reached out and petted my fletching, or my aim was off an inch or two, compounded with jumping the string, it would be asking for a gut or liver shot. I've made more challenging shots before, but my little voice said "No."

I learned a long time ago if you don't heed, the results could or will be disastrous. Of awesome shots I've made before, like threading the eye of a needle, it was done almost involuntarily. Most of the time I didn't even remember aiming. So, if you catch yourself contemplating for several seconds trying to reassure yourself on an iffy shot, don't take it. The buck resumed his chasing for another 30 minutes or so until the does had had enough and broke off in single file, following the old nanny lead doe toward their bedding area for the day. Awesome. Knight & Hale pulled him off the real thing.

No worry, plenty of time. I've already got three does in the freezer from opening week. At this point, I've passed up more than a dozen small bucks. I could've shot some more does, but I have to leave some for rut bait. In this area, there are at least two noticeable ruts. In the same area last season in late December, there were three big bucks each paired with their own doe, and breeding was observed. It was a comical morning.

One doe was in her peak and was stopping for mounting throughout the chasing venue. The buck would clumsily rear up and slip slide down by her side causing her to nervously jump out of the way, and the chase would begin again until the next pause. Why was he so clumsy? Because, he had only three legs. Of course, he doesn't need any of them now, THUMP!

I watched this deer for longer than an hour — boy, deer surely are the ultimate adapters. You couldn't even tell he had three legs.

I won't be returning here to hunt until Nov. 18-20, hopefully timing when the first rut hits and all the heavy hitters are in town. Maybe Tripod left some of his genes behind. I got to go "hunt on the fly" now to some more WMAs that are date sensitive.

## Nov. 7: Horse Creek WMA

I'm 1 mile deep into the Ocmulgee River swamp floodplain in an old swampy clearcut. I'm hunting ugly along a narrow, thick ridge funneling from the thick clearcut ending out into a more open floodplain. There's a dim trail down the center with plenty of rubs. I forgot my limb saw.

All I needed was 12 feet — any higher and visibility would be cut. I couldn't find a limbless section anywhere. I should have stayed there OTG, but instead I found a climbable tree on the outer edge of the thick run. I made a little noise getting up the tree; it was harder than a railroad spike. I hurriedly hit the rattle bag and shook some limbs.

A few minutes later I heard a buck thrashing a bush with his antlers, and by the tone he had some serious bone on his head. The buck was just out of sight in the center of the funnel and wouldn't come any closer. I knew it wasn't going to happen. He was right on top of my entry trail, which was screened from my view. If I had only brought that limb saw or went OTG. A golden rule of hunting and little voices — stick with your first choice even if you have to adapt. I wonder how big that headgear was.....

## Nov. 8-10: Dixon Memorial WMA

This is my favorite hunt, and its check-in, meaning bonus tags. I'm hunting buck, doe and bear in and around the Okefenokee Swamp. This place has a deep and mysterious magnetism that draws me every year. Maybe it's my Indian heritage. There are places here where no modern-day hunter has ever set foot. It's 32,000 acres where you can discover your own little world of hunting tranquility. The deer are in full rut, and several big bucks have been killed. I found many running tracks and even found scrapes in the dirt road. On this either-sex hunt, 44 deer were killed with a success rate in the mid-20s. I hunted with friend David Rodriquez of Homestead, Fla.

## Nov. 8: A.M. Hunt:

We were unproductive in a usually productive honey hole. The difference was this time there were no hunters in front of or around the block like there usually are. We need 'em to push deer to security cover, which is in the form of a thick cypress swamp with knee-deep water. Where's a crowd when you need one? Doesn't sound like a sane hunter talking, does it? Remember, people move, deer move — especially on that first pressured day. A rub line by my tree was not reworked this year. I killed a nice 5 1/2-year-old 8-pointer here last year. It must have been his.

## Nov. 8 P.M. Hunt:

We found a lot of fresh deer sign, including scrapes, on a maintained road. Deer are coming out of a thick pine-palmetto flat, crossing the road into a young clearcut with reset pines where they have been feeding and chasing at night. Behind the narrow pine and palmetto block is a large ty-ty swamp with several worn trails coming out at every bend and dip. Take a pick. Rubs and scrapes dotted the access trail between the flat and ty-ty bay. With wind in our favor, David and I picked a spot. Nothing. They may be getting there late at night. Anyhow, deer don't appear to be moving in the evenings this quarter of the moon.

Nov. 9 A.M. Hunt:

I had an idea what the deer may be doing, so I drove a mile around to the back of the block. We crossed, but more like bulldozed through, a huge pine-palmetto flat to the back side of the same ty-ty swamp. Most people wouldn't have left all that pretty sign, but I'm not ordinary. Twenty-five years of hunting public land and your predatory instinct will take over — trust me. From any road it was about as deep as you could get, at least 3/4 of a mile out to either end of the firebreak where it meets the road.

We hunted on each side of a long, looping point of the swamp which jutted out into the head-high flat of palmettos and gallberry bushes, which is prime bedding area with browse.

I have learned deer like to bed after crossing some sort of obstacle or change in terrain. It may be a road, a stream or swamp, a wide-open field, changes in thickness of cover or maybe just something different. For some reason, that gives them a sense of security. As hunters and the hunted, we are all looking for that fresh undisturbed block. This turned out to be a good choice.

I like going blind in a new area. This is where your GPS comes in really handy. Sometimes you can't read it from the road. My Garmin allowed us to center up that 1 1/2-mile stretch for the area of least disturbance. There were several other sets of boot tracks coming in from each end of the break, but those petered out after a quarter-mile or so, leaving that juicy little spot in the middle. Surprise 'em — first time in is the best time. No residual scent or disturbance left from prior scouting — no warning.

We heard several grunting sequences in the back side of the bay, and soon after the scent of gunpowder filled the air. We bagged two spikes and a doe which will surely hide the bottom of our freezers. David's spike and doe were shot in the access trail, coming out of the ty-ty swamp heading to their presumed sanctuary. He dropped them in their tracks on each side of a small secondary point behind his side of the loop. Both were actually lying half in and half out of the firebreak and swamp.

My spike came out of the bedding side only minutes after I'd had a coughing fit which was hurriedly followed up with one heck of a rattle-bag tantrum and grunting that would scare a moose to death. Like turkey calling, never finish on a bad note. Disguise your mistakes.

My spike came out in a little recess where a small oak had fallen across the trail, creating a shield from the flat to the swamp. Just like bass, these deer were relating to structure in their movements such as using points, dips, changes in cover and terrain, and connection paths. Think about it; a reservoir is flooded woods just like we are hunting today. To me, structure (underwater) and terrain (dry land) are basically the same, so I apologize if I use fishing terminology while writing this. I think we did a pretty good job reading the structure in the dark by finding the subtle differences within it.

Drifting back to the subject, instead of bedding in or running perpendicular within the ty-ty bay farther down to exit, these deer were just going straight across to the back bedroom in the pines. Every one of these deer had their own little slip-out spot, and all paused, peering out before crossing the narrow firebreak, exposing only up to their front shoulder.

PEEK-A-BOOM!

Nov. 9: P.M. Hunt

We figured the a.m. hunt pretty much boogered up our new honeyhole for the remainder of the day due to all the hide sledding and sweating for a mile. We were still all smiles after running the gallberry gauntlet. We tried a couple of experimental overlooked areas near the road that evening. Nothing seen or heard but one distant shot. Again, deer don't seem to be moving much in the evenings.

Nov. 10: A.M. Hunt

I moved a couple hundred yards down from the area where our previous successful a.m. hunt was. I hunted in the middle of a series of short, snakelike bends in ankle-deep water. I had to climb higher than 30 feet to catch a couple of bends in the firebreak and to find a few openings in the flat, which was well over head high in gallberries and palmettos. My tree sure did skinny up quick — end result was shaky. My little voice said if I was presented with a shot, raise my gun slowly so I wouldn't rock my world.

About 8 a.m. I glimpsed two does, or should I say two doe heads, browsing out in the tall gallberries. Already crossed and bedded in there well before daylight, huh? For the next few minutes all I watched was mostly ears and patches of brown. Unless I was wanting to join Shaky Bush Hunting Club, I was going to have to pray for an ethical opening. And there it was, a brief pause in a wide opening. I raised my rifle up quickly for a time-constrained shot. You dummy, remember the little voice?

The deer took a big hop and looked back over its shoulder. Big mistake! I did a quick spin going into a Yoga move, throwing my leg up high over the rail for a prop. A big pop and a drop. You must become one with your equipment grasshopper. David and I were both limited out on deer now. We concluded our hunt in the edge of the Big Swamp over some fresh bear tracks. I didn't really expect to see one, but it was a great way to end the hunt by having some quiet time to reflect on our success while enjoying the majestic beauty and aura this swamp possesses. Even the smells will tweak something deep down inside of you. Blow, Blow Seminole Wind!

My hunting partner for the past three days speaks very little English, and I don't speak Spanish. It made for an interesting hunt. His compadres and also my fellow hunting on the fly associates, Armando and Ernesto, who both speak English, have been hunting Georgia WMAs for 27 years. There was a lot of sign language. We quickly found out the language we both understood was deer hunting. Even though it was a tough hunt and we didn't get a big rutting buck, it was well worthwhile in the end with the sparkling eyes, ear-to-ear big grinning smile and a parting hug when he said, "Mucho happy, my friend."

It was a very special hunt for some other friends present at this hunt also. Paul Minter of Waynesville's 17-year-old daughter, Heather, killed a doe, her first deer. How sweet it is! I really respect Paul for taking the time to scout and place stands for his daughters even if it means sacrificing his own hunt time. I've seen him drag ladder stands in and out morning, midday and evening every day of the hunt, keeping his daughters in fresh spots if earlier ones are unproductive.

But as a father and a husband, I, too, would rather see my loved ones more successful than myself. For me, it's like getting to hunt two or three places at the same time. It really helps out on my 50/50/90 rule. When I have a 50/50 chance of choosing the deer's route, 90 percent of the time I'm wrong. Friend Tim Griffin, also of Waynesville, killed a 4 1/2-year-old 8-point buck, a really good 'un for this part of the state. He was hunting on the edge of a travel route along a small swamp, less than 100 yards from the road. It's one of those overlooked spots everybody drives right by.

His hunt was very special, because he had just come out of the hospital from having heart bypass and pacemaker surgery days earlier. His nickname will be "Iron Man" from now on. Hunting must be part of his own recovery plan. The spirit heals, both physical and within. If you love to hunt, you can feel it when you get out into the woods. Awesome!

Nov. 12: Flat Tub WMA

A.M. Hunt:

This is a highly pressured WMA, which is open the majority of the season. Hunting OTG today, checking on four waypoints posted last year on my Garmin. These are very hidden and thick out-of-the-way spots in an area of small pines and briar thickets. A couple of narrow brush-choked hardwood drains, more like ravines, separate the various plantations.

At the four locations I found two ladder stands, chop trails, repetitive climbing marks on the trees I had chose and a gut pile. Somebody else beat me to 'em all. It took me a lot of scouting late last season to lay out a battle plan for this year, but if you snooze, you lose. Whoever it was, they were good at scouting and stand placement. There was also evidence of overhunting — got to get out of here.

Nov. 13: Flat Tub WMA

Returned for more punishment. OTG. Stalked through the center of a large jungle of briars and small pines in the heart of the WMA. I was hopscotching the freshest sign along a myriad of deer trails. There was nothing beat down as far as tracks, just a lot of repetitive coming and going. There were several scrapes scattered along but no clusters or fresh rubs. The sign was most likely summer trails and/or exodus highways when changing primary food sources to other portions of the WMA. Judging by the sign, it was probably just a couple of small bucks coming through here every few days while working a circuitous route for hot does.

A lot of these trails tend to curve out toward private property, but I stayed in center of block via GPS, cutting as many trails as I could, like a rut-mobile buck.

Several hours and over a mile later of unblinking tension, I came out the other end of the block. Nothing. I landed in an access trail only yards from a major parking and dispersal area for the New York Marathon, judging by the multitude of boot tracks.

I stepped around a small curve, pulled my face mask off, uh-oh. I was eyeball to eyeball, busted. A doe was standing broadside 50 yards away, wide open in the trail where she is definitely, positively not supposed to be.

Awww, come on now! After a grueling mile of de-thorning bushels of briars in a hopeful mecca of whitetails, this was heart-wrenching. Lil' voice even told me to peek around the corner- but shoooot, not here, not now. Well, here goes the same old drill.

I slowly raise my gun, touch my cheekbone to the stock, look through the scope, and the split second before I can focus and squeeze, the deer takes off like a freakin' rocket. I did follow the deer with the scope for a few seconds but passed on the shot. You won today. Must have been one of those adrenaline-junkie deer counting coup on yet another humbled hunter.

Nov. 12: Little Satilla WMA

P.M. Hunt:

Hunting on the Fly, driving two hours round trip for just an afternoon hunt. Unbeknownst to me, timber harvesting had left broad skidder trails through what was once my (sorry Don, I mean our) honeyhole in a little ty-ty strip. There's litter everywhere with way too much presence of hunter sign.

It's run-and-gun time, checking on back-up spots. I ended the day stalking in a small pine thicket near the road.

Nothing. I'll be back this summer to scout. There is always a productive spot waiting to be found. Remember it only takes one to be successful.

## Nov. 14: Horse Creek WMA

I was doing some in-season scouting for the upcoming check-in hunt. Long distance walk-in areas along the river where I usually hunt were hit hard from last week's sign-in hunt. I decided to look for some short pockets near the road that would be overlooked by most hunters. I love to experiment while eliminating ground.

I found a few areas possessing the key elements — it must be unappealing to hunters, thick for bedding, ample deer sign and it must have at least abundant browse, so they won't have to leave during daylight hours. Sometimes you can go in too deep, missing out on a few of these cagey survivors. I located two corner lots in a narrow rectangular block. Both possessed the elements I look for, reading the spots only from the road.

## Nov. 15: A.M. Hunt:

The morning spot didn't pan out.

## Nov. 15: P.M. Hunt:

The evening spot almost felt silly with a road encircling three sides of me less than 100 yards away. I even did a few wiggle-finger waves at some astonished drive-byers. I could almost hear 'em saying, "Look at that idiot right by the road."

I climbed higher than 40 feet up. I'm not required to have a pilot's license, am I? I still didn't have much visibility into the thicket. At least my scent was blowing into the next county.

A few minutes before dark three does emerged from the cover. They staged in a small opening and began preening and scent checking while waiting on dark. I watched their body language a few minutes for clues of a lagging suitor (buck), but it was quickly approaching dark.

I felt like dragging something, so I took out the lead doe and left the rest for seed. The drag to the road was so short. I started to do it again just so my back muscles wouldn't feel cheated. This is a future hot spot for deer until it gets noticed. Park far away when hunting places like this.

There were beds everywhere in the tall gallberries and ty-ty bushes. In the center of the strip is a miniscule drain that makes a natural funnel into the bedding area. I can't wait to try it one morning next season. I knew it would probably be better as a morning spot, but I took a gamble because it was a real windy day and the only place I could find with the wind in my favor.

I'm going to write an article one day called "Cutting Corners for Big Bucks," ha ha! Deer (hogs, too) love to cut corners, sometimes several, when covering ground for estrus females. They'll cut trails to throw off predators and check points for hunter intrusion, such as visible traffic and parked mechanical scent bombs.

Gotta swing wide and look up.

Nov. 16: Horse Creek WMA

A.M. Hunt:

I remembered a swamp-finger drain from last year. I found lots of big rubs lining the inner edge, just like last year, but nothing fresh. They must be sniffing somewhere else now. A large bobcat found my entry trail and crept to the base of my tree. From 40 feet, I spit on his head three times. Pretty good, huh? Left puzzled. No deer seen.

Hunting on the Fly

# Chapter 7
## Suwannee River Warmouth

By Glen Solomon
Published by *GON* on May 30, 2019

Fishing for panfish on the west side of the Okefenokee Swamp.

Tap, tap! The underwater thumps on my little plastic 4-inch offering resonated down the graphite rod to my hand.

I pointed the rod tip to the water, took up the dip in the line, and drove the thin-wired, razor sharp 1/0 Gamakatsu home. Shortly after crossing his eyes, and sharp as a ray of sunshine shooting through a hole in a cloud, a gold belly rolled to the top of the black tannic water. It'll be the first thing you notice on a strawberry perch, also known as a warmouth, when the surface breaks.

As most fish in waters fed by the Okefenokee Swamp, their backs and upper sides will be dark brown to black. Once in your hand, a compliment of many other colors on its sides will appear, mottled and polka-dotted together in a digital camo pattern.

The opening scenario above didn't happen once but dozens of times throughout a recent day of fishing on the river. My friend, Donald Wood, of Brunswick, accompanied me here for his first trip to the beginning leg of the Suwannee formed by the Okefenokee Swamp. All but 35 of the 246-mile Suwannee River flows in Florida, but in my opinion, Georgia has the very best stretch for fishing and enjoying its beauty, a wild remoteness undefiled by civilization.

I've been coming here off and on for more than 40 years, so this river is definitely entombed in my heritage, and I'll use any opportunity to share my love for it.

That afternoon, we hurriedly set up camp at Lem Griffis Fish Camp, located on Highway 177 on the left just before the entrance into Stephen Foster State Park. The park is one of the gateways to the expansive and unique Okefenokee Swamp. The park is a wonderful place to stay, as well, with a lot of amenities to offer. However, at Griffis Fish Camp, I feel more harmonic in a sense, blending peacefully with the quietness, remoteness and a deeper feeling of one with nature. Once you walk under the camp's live oaks, a trip down the shady lane to the camp's launch site on the white sands of the Suwannee, you'll feel the magnetism, as well.

Griffis offers water and electrical hook-ups, bathrooms, showers and a screened porch with a chimney fireplace. Launch fee is $2 per boat, whether you launch or take out there. Some anglers will do float trips and only take-out at Griffis ramp.

Above the Griffis ramp, and just inside Stephen Foster State Park, you can turn left onto Suwannee River Sill Road and access a ramp on the right that will allow you to access to the headwaters of the Suwannee River. This ramp is only a few miles above the Griffis pay launch site and gives you ample time to fish between the two points.

For more info on the <u>Griffis Fish Camp</u>, call Al Griffis at (912) 637-5289.

*Glen Solomon with a very nice Suwannee River warmouth.*

If you have time during your visit, sit a spell with Mr. Griffis and have a chat of swamp tales of long ago. No one is better informed about the history and folklore of the area. Check out his little museum full of artifacts, memorabilia and old taxidermy work. Al's father, Lem Griffis, was well-known for his writings, spinning yarns and tall tales in the early and mid-20th century while running this camp until his death in 1968. Google the name and enjoy what I dubbed the "Jerry Clower of the Swamp."

My grandfather fished this area a lot. He drowned in the Suwannee in 1970. He was probably good friends with Lem Griffis. I was only 3 years old then and never accompanied him, so I find it amazing that I was drawn here as well, and I inadvertently began carrying on a family tradition.

"Most people picture the Swamp as being a stagnant place and a drainage basin full of muck," said Al Griffis. "But to the contrary, the Okefenokee is at a higher elevation than the surrounding areas. It's descending flow spawns two of the cleanest rivers in the state, the Suwannee and the St. Mary's. Pure and healthy waters without any residue build-up or environmental issues such as pollution from big factories or run-off from metropolitan areas."

I'm thinking maybe that's why all these fish taste so good.

That evening we put in at the concrete boat ramp on Suwannee River Sill Road. Driving toward the ramp, the adjoining woods on the sides of the river were teeming with deer and longbearded gobblers like we were at a petting zoo. They even gobbled as we left the ramp.

It was already after 6 p.m., so we planned just to fish a short distance downriver. The river was on the low side, exposing the beautiful white sand banks and dry swamp floodplains.

One purpose of this trip was to find out if a new-found lure was just as awesome here as it was on the east side of the Swamp at the Suwannee Canal near Folkston. I made three trips there this year, and I absolutely tore up the warmouth, catching limits in less than a couple hours. It beat live worms, crickets and small crawfish that friends, seasoned locals and I used comparatively on the same trips. It's not the Suwannee River on the east side, but we'd be fishing the same water that is fed directly from the Big Swamp and has the exact swamp fish present.

The float would be a test run for the long-planned day tomorrow. My rig consisted of a Lew's Speed Spool baitcaster and a 5-6 Berkley Lightning rod spooled with 12-lb. Big Game mono. A double Trilene knot attached my green-pumpkin 4-inch plastic worm. Don had two Zebco ultralight spincasts, lined with 8-lb. Seaguar fluorocarbon and set up on 5-foot Blaze rods, one rigged with a crawfish-colored 1/8-oz. Satilla Spin and the other with a 1/32-oz. white red dot Beetle Spin, both proven lures here.

Just downriver past the first cut-off on the right which circles back to the Sill, our first targets of tree-lined banks began. Because of the low river level, it was mostly a myriad of root systems spreading into the black water. The area was mainly tupelos with a few cypresses spread along, which would have their strands of cypress knees jutting into the water, resembling the top of a dinosaur's back.

*Don Wood, of Brunswick, recently took his first trip to the upper section of the Suwannee River.*

It didn't take but a couple of casts before I felt that familiar thump that so many bass worm fisherman are familiar with. My pulse did a double-pump, slack line take-up, rear back and BAM! A tight line and a bent rod. Fatty warmouth in the boat. Inside his huge maw for such a little fish, the plastic bait was coiled neatly in a circle, and the entire thin wire 1/0 Gamakatsu was engulfed, as well. Man, they love that little worm. It's soft and designed so that it collapses well. It's spongy and salty tasting, so they will hold on to it. What surprises me is the bite to hook-up ratio is in the upper 90% range. Using a baitcaster and bass gear for panfish, who'd figure?

In the next few yards, the little worm picked up several more. Past the second opening of a small lake on the right, the shaded banks began again, and we picked up at least two dozen more warmouth and two hand-sized stumpknockers. Don was bringing up the rear with the Satilla Spin and was absolutely hammering the bluegill, stumpknockers and an occasional warmouth. As far as warmouth, he was fishing used water. The little green-pumpkin worm was seining ahead of him.

We stopped 200 hundred yards downriver, knowing the river section was going to be prime in the morning. We would put in at Griffis and fish up to this area. We went back upstream to the first turn-off I mentioned earlier.

Try this area. Face upstream and within sight of the break in the cement flood gate on the sill. The downstream side entering is the best side. It's a little deeper and provides more shade. This is a hot spot for chain pickerel. My favorite lure for them are Dura-Spins and a topwater wood prop bait called a Zip 'n Sam, handcrafted by Sam Griffin. For now, both Don and I were focusing on warmouth, catching a few more nice ones at that spot.

As you progress around the curve to the right and through a straight run portion, there will be a short slough spur to the right. The banks to the left and right at the junction are two more jackfish hotspots.

If you can't find a Zip 'n Sam or Dura-Spin, I've also did well with similar prop baits, such as a Devil Horse or a Dying Flutter. Dura-Spins can be found in many South Georgia tackle stores. Satilla Marine in Waycross has a huge assortment of Zips. Otherwise they can be ordered. I always bring several different Dura-Spins, as there always seem to be a daily preference of the fish, whether being a change of skirt or blade color.

As you enter this little slough, the warmouth becomes ruler here. The right bank was the ticket when we fished, especially where the large cypress trees are out from the bank. Don and I caught several of the bucketmouth slabs on each side of it. At the left-hand curve ahead, the outside bend is a deeper pool, where we gathered some more large ones. This is also a great catfish hole. Simply drop a live worm or a piece of shrimp. These yellow bullhead catfish from the Suwannee and the Swamp are the tastiest I've eaten anywhere in the state.

We stopped fishing for the evening at that point, ready to get back to camp and rest for the knowingly beautiful day tomorrow. We caught and released approximately 40 to 50 panfish, primarily warmouth, not bad for 1 1/2 hours.

At 7 the next morning, we launched from the launch site on the campground property, dropping the trolling motor and immediately beginning to fish. Being I couldn't get Don to throw anything else but the little plastic worm now, I picked up the Satilla Spin. On my second, third and fifth casts I put two bluegill and a large stumpknocker in the boat. Don soon caught a couple nice warmouth, which prompted me to pick up my worm rod for our primary target of the day.

Every tree or trash pile we tossed to had at least a couple of warmouth on it. A lot of trees were out of the water, but their countless roots and tussock mats fed well out into the water. After a couple hours, we noticed the larger 1/2- to nearly 1-lb. warmouth were coming off the very last tree right before a mudflat, sandbar or slough opening. Also, the warmouth seemed oblivious to any disturbance of the boat, catching many with a short toss only a few feet away. This is how I caught our biggest warmouth of the day on one of those last trees before a flatwater section.

Another tip for fishing here is to work the worm all the way back to the boat if you don't get hit near the bank cover. The fish may be a few yards out in the river if current and deeper water is present. Unlike bass where most strikes will be on the fall or the first drag, warmouth will hit it all the way back to the rod tip, so work it patiently if the spot looks good. They'll even hit it dead-sticked on the bottom.

*Glen Solomon's recent trip to the Suwannee River included 60 panfish (mostly warmouth), six jackfish, two bass and several bowfin and chain pickerel.*

By 2 p.m., the bite had slowed, and we figured we had enough warmouth for the day. Don was ready for a swim back at the landing since the sun had been relentless.

However, before taking a dip in the Suwannee, we had to see if the jack (chain pickerel) and bowfin wanted to eat. You can usually count on at least one of them biting when the sun is beaming and the air is steaming. I release all bowfin, but I always keep a few jacks.

Other than the butter cats (yellow bullheads), they are the tastiest fish of the bunch. Simply make quarter-inch gashes apart the length of the fish, fry and enjoy those big white flaky chunks.

While covering water fast with Dura-Spins, I caught two small bowfin and lost a huge one on the Dura-Spin, but the jacks were hitting with a fury. They offer very exciting strikes as they'll hit wide open and fast, often becoming airborne. These toothy missiles will put on the most acrobatic fight of all the swamp species and are very fun to catch. Reel as fast as you can, keep pressure and use a stiff rod because they will sling those treble hooks back at you.

In the next few minutes I caught six and had several of the hard-tooths sling my lure out. The last one weighed 2.29 pounds and ended the day. Well, that and a dip in the river.

Tally for the trip taken home was more than 60 panfish (mostly warmouth), six jackfish and two bass. Add in the bowfin and several bass released, we had a 100-plus fish day.

Besides the Suwannee Sill Landing, there is another public landing located just out of Fargo on 441 South.

Please be aware that if you put in at the Sill, there is a 10-hp limit for a short distance down the river, which is the portion inside the Okefenokee Wildlife Refuge. There will be signage posted.

# Chapter 8
## Public-Land Hog Hunting in August

By Glen Solomon
Published by *GON* on August 3, 2018

Yep, sure is hot. August is always a scorcher. But, how much do you love hunting? Aug. 15 is the opening day of WMA squirrel season, and wild hogs are also legal to take. I consider this to be the easiest time to fill my freezer with wild pork or bag a trophy boar.

In answer to the above, I do love hunting enough to brave the heat, further enhanced by the fact that WMA hogs have been left alone for nearly three months. A calmer animal is easier to hunt. Because of the heat, they can be easier to pinpoint as they will be drawn to the cooler swamps, drainages and floodplains to wallow and lay up. If a high and dry food source is a good distance away, they will have a very defined travel corridor, there and back. Cut across some fresh sign, and track 'em down.

Covering ground, runnin' and gunnin' WMAs has always been my favorite hog strategy. We have a lot of WMAs with hogs, some loaded, some less, and some with hogs on occasion.

*Brandon Beasley of Oak Park.*

Brandon Beasley, of Oak Park, arrowed this nice 120-lb. Di-Lane WMA boar on May 30 despite the eradication of more than 400 hogs on Di-Lane and the surrounding area by federal shooters in a helicopter. Brandon likes to stalk the many hardwood and pine flats on Di-Lane. Keeping the wind in his favor and following the freshest sign, he will pay special attention to any thickets along the way. This is where the hogs will be bedded when they're not feeding nearby or en route to one of the many dove fields or adjacent agricultural lands. The trip before his success, he actually found them bedded in a thicket in the middle of a fairly open area. The wind wasn't in his favor, so he backed out. He returned a few days later, found the wind in his favor and resumed the stalk. As he neared the thicket, he smelled the hogs. Brandon said, "CLOSE! The bushes started shaking, and I heard a couple moving off. I waited for 10 minutes as I knew more were in there. I eased around the next bush, and there stood one looking right at me. I let the arrow fly, and he crashed 30 yards away."

Over the years I've been successful and have accumulated a list of waypoints that I now check every August. Hogs are either there or they're not. If present, I put the ol' Indian stalk on 'em. If not, I'll keep moving to the next spot or next WMA.

Go all day. I've taken many hogs at midday, with many of them on the move feeding. Others bedded or perhaps in a wallow, which is a great midday spot. Get on sign, and follow it.

Preparation is going to be key this time of year. You need to cover ground efficiently and comfortably. Here are my key essentials for hog hunting WMAs in August.

145

Ice Water: Hydrate well before the hunt. Take plenty of water with you, and have some cold drinks at the truck when you return.

GPS and Extra Batteries: No time for being lost. Knowing the most direct route back out is crucial.

Backpack: Inside will be bottled water, cleaning knife, latex gloves and large ice bags to store meat, so I don't bloody up my backpack. Learn to quarter out meat on the ground at the kill site. It's too hot to be dragging all that extra weight around. You'll be needing to get your meat on ice quickly.

ThermaCell and Skeeter Spray: A must. You may not always need these, but when you do, they are hunt savers.
Extra Tees: You will be getting sweated down. A fresh shirt feels wonderful.

This year on May 16-31, we had our first WMA coyote/feral hog season. Being that I like to do articles with fresh photos, this would be my only opportunity to do a run on several WMAs before the August season opener. With only two weekends during the short 16-day season and folks tuned more into May fishing, I knew it would be a challenge. I recruited a few WMA hitmen, and off we went. On the following three pages are the results of those efforts. Each successful hunter offered up a photo and their hunt story. These stories are designed to teach you something and give you success in August.

By looking at all the pictures and information, it looks like we have a lot to look forward to on many WMAs. Hope to see y'all hunting on the fly in August.

If you need any advice or help, give me a holler at huntingonthefly@yahoo.com.

Josh Stapler, of Bowdon, with a Hannahatchee WMA three-footed hog he took on May 26. Josh and his friend Shane Turpen located some fresh sign and rootings in an area, set up a ground blind and waited them out. A large group of hogs soon approached with a large boar bringing up the rear. The one above neared their blind a little too close. This August, Josh or Shane, show us that 300-lb. boar!

Dale Anderson, of Callahan, Fla, with a trio of Griffin Ridge WMA hogs taken on May 19. The author guided him to the HAT Honey Hole. Stalking in unison, the pair quickly caught up to a group of hogs rooting slowly along the funnel spot of a lengthy travel corridor. Learned from past experiences, this is the route hogs use when swapping ends of the WMA, which lies along the Altamaha River corridor. This particular funnel spot is a narrow hardwood flat between the main river and a large bay swamp. The acronym HAT stands for Hogs Always There. Any takers for August? Then, the squirrels will start cutting the early overcup acorns in the tops, which leaves a lot of crumb residue and the dropped acorns they bit and tested. That will attract even more hogs and stall others as they travel through.

Mark Williams, of Blackshear, with a fine gilt taken at Dixon Memorial WMA. By staying on the move checking multiple spots where he'd seen rooting sign in the past, Mark crossed paths with a large group of hogs. With open cover and the wind right, he waited until they fed into some tall sawgrass before stalking and finished up with a shot at a mere 10 yards. Mark kept his nose to the grindstone, even with the sun up and getting hot. Mark hunts the contour edges of the main Okefenokee Swamp and is aware they will feed at any time of the day.

Lucky Beasley, Brandon Beasley and Ron Shaw, of Oak Park, enjoy preparing the rewards of their WMA May sausage run.

The author with a midday hog taken at Big Hammock WMA on May 25. He reports, "Fresh sign was all over the area, but it was of little amount, just where one to three hogs pilfered through and wouldn't return. Apparently food was scarce, only to consist of worms, grubs, bugs, grass roots, rotten acorns, etc. They were surviving by constantly searching, meaning you had to get ahead of these hogs or walk your tail off until you bump into one. It took three morning hunts, but I finally gridded off enough ground to meet up with three of the ghosts alongside a slough rim, just shy of a thick bamboo run. August will be a lot better, as there will be a few early live oaks falling. Squirrels will start cutting in the tops of the other oaks (white, water and pin) that will soon drop on their own in September. Find those early acorn trees with cuttings or acorns under them. If there's any hog sign, check morning, midday and evening. If no success on the oak trees, check the nearest palmetto patches (hill or swamp), high bluff banks along the river with willows and canegrass and the swampiest sections around the many interior oxbow lakes. The morning after a good thunderstorm is a great time to find hogs, as it blows acorns out the trees, and these rooters are easier to track.

Steven McCumbers, of Hazlehurst, with a Flat Tub WMA trio of two gilts and a young boar taken on May 20. He began a long phenomenal stalk, tracking the hogs across an entire half-mile block, running slam out of woods. He crossed a dirt road, picked up the sign and continued across a dry pinch point of a river slough into a 6-acre block of chest-high bamboo grass. After a 100 yards or so, he soon heard rustling in the thick cover. They were bedded in there for the day and were now milling about, only 20 yards away. With very few openings and the wind right, he opted to wait as evening was fast approaching. Forty-five minutes later, the hogs made their move. When the first one popped out, he took quick aim and dropped it. As the second one burst out right before him, he killed him. Hearing noise to the side, he spun and hip-shot another one at only 3 yards.

Ron Shaw, of Oak Park, with a fine Tuckahoe hog taken by bow on May 18. At midday, Ron checked a known wallow site, found some real fresh sign and began back-tracking. Crossing a road, he followed the sign until he caught up with them in their bedding area. They had just risen to feed and were coming in his direction. Being caught in a semi-open area, he squatted to his knees and came to full draw. He held anchor for over two minutes. The larger hogs were bringing up the rear. One of the smaller ones had come within 15 yards and then started to turn away. Ron could judge by body language that it was about to bolt, which would scatter them all. Taking careful aim at the lead hog, Thwack!

Mark Williams with his second May hog, this one from Penholoway Swamp WMA on May 23. The author and Mark were hopping islands by boat off the Altamaha River. Mark reports, "Stalking along the mud-covered oak flat without making noise was easy enough. Doing so without squatting mosquitoes, not so much. As I eased along keeping the wind in my face, I was intentional on stopping every three to four steps to look for movement but also to listen. An hour into my hunt, I caught movement to my upward left. It was a mature black boar slipping along a much swampier area. I propped up against a nearby oak and waited for a window of opportunity in the nasty fringe of cover which lay along the muddy backwaters of a flooded slough. Seconds later, the hog stopped broadside, and I sent a well-placed .270 round into his shoulder."

Hunting on the Fly

# Chapter 9
## GON Hunt Advisory Team Reports

By Glen Solomon
Published in various editions of GON

**Glen Solomon's Reports as a Member of the Georgia Outdoor News Hunt Advisory Team**

(**Editor's Note:** Glen made the following reports over several years as he served on the Georgia Outdoor News Hunt Advisory Team used by the magazine to inform readers of activities around the state.)

**December 2008**

Telfair Co.: Glen Solomon has this report from the Horse Creek WMA hunts Nov. 5-8 and Nov. 13-15: "On the WMA hunts I attended this November, the rut has been more awesome and noticeable than in past years. I've heard several people state this same comment the last couple of weeks, 'He had his nose right up her rear!' All phases of the rut have been observed such as chasing, scent-trailing, pairing up in small areas of thick cover and even breeding.

On the last hunt Nov. 13-15, some parts of the WMA had scrapes staying fresh and cleaned out, while on other portions of the WMA they were collecting leaves. Thank God they have another hunt in December; this thing I believe is gonna string on out — not just a trickle rut either. There were several nice 8-pointers with 16-inch spreads and better, including a 19-incher. Some were reported even bigger than that on the prior hunt the week before, which had a success rate in the 30 percent ranges. This week was in the 20s even though it was a back-to-back hunt. They'll kick tail in the GON rankings next year. I had two chances at a real good 'un after he exited his bedding area, and I blew it both times. I will have him surrounded on the December hunt. It was a check-in hunt and the start of freezer-filling time, so the meat hunter in me bagged a spike OTG and the heaviest doe of the hunt.

*Glen with a nice 8 at the Horse Creek WMA sign in Telfair County.*

In August, Glen Solomon and his wife, Cindy, hunted Griffin Ridge WMA for three days and killed five hogs. "There actually weren't many hogs on the area," said Glen. "We put 22 miles on our boots in those three days." Five hogs in three days is a pile of pork, but the Solomans had to work much harder to find the hogs.

## January 2009

WMAs: Glenn Solomon reports: "The last couple of weeks I've been hunting "On the Fly" chasing this rut thing all over the state. I've been to Penholoway, Dixon Memorial, Horse Creek, Oaky Woods and Walter F. George. Scored on all as far as meat is concerned, except at Oaky Woods in Houston and Pulaski counties Dec. 3-6, which will probably be one of the best hunts for the year in terms of hunter success and trophy bucks. I was only there for a couple of days, but man, they were slaying big bucks left and right. The rut was wide open with cruising bucks getting shot in the open areas like the powerline right-of-ways. I guess I overhunted by being in the small pine and briar thickets. At Horse Creek in Telfair County Dec. 11-13, they had another awesome hunt. Three more large bucks were killed, including a 220-lb. 12-pointer. On Dec. 16, I watched two 8-points with does at Walter F. George in Quitman County — swollen neck and dark hock glands on the one I grunted in within 10 yards. Fresh rubs were all over the hillside. They are just getting cranked up here, again! My friend, Eddie Watson of Clay Hill Hunting Preserve a few miles down the road, said he's been noticing the rut extending into February and even early March. I think the rut still starts at the normal times in respective areas but tends to string out through the entire season and even a couple of months thereafter, depending on the weather and moon phases. All the does are not getting bred in a short window like everybody thinks. So if you're reading this, chunk it down and get your camo-clad booty out there. It ain't over till it's over! All it takes is that one hot doe for a taxidermy bill!"

**Oct 2009**

Brantley County: Glen Solomon reports that his buddy Paul Minter, of Waynesville, arrowed a doe at Little Satilla WMA. "He's a handicapped hunter who doesn't let his disability slow his love of hunting. I hadn't talked to him in detail about his adventure yet, but he texted me some interesting messages — he's a multi-task hunter too...

8:07 p.m: lookin 4 doe shot at Little Satilla…. 8:25 p.m: found blood, gone 300 yards now… 8:27 p.m.: arrow still in deer… 8:35 p.m: just found tip of arrow…. 8:59 p.m: found my deer!!!'

"Congrats buddy!"

*Glen leaning on his truck with a nice 8-point.*

**Oct 2009**

Jeff Davis County: Glen Solomon hunted Bullard Creek WMA the second week of the season. "I got to hunt after expecting to be on the road working. I hadn't taken the time to find any food sources because I thought I was going to be out of state, so I opted to hunt a bedding area of a big buck we've been after a couple years. I saw five very large does at 9 a.m., and strangely none of them had any fawns with them. Coyotes perhaps?

"After talking to a dozen or more folks and enacting the public-land hunting grapevine, it appears for the most part deer didn't move too well in the daylight heat to feed. The folks sitting on food sources such as water-oak acorns and persimmons didn't report seeing anything, only those hunting in or near bedding areas."

*Glen with a small 8-point.*

# Chapter 10
## 60 Days of Extreme WMA Hog Hunting

By Glen Solomon
Published by *GON* on December 23, 2007

Most Georgia WMAs are open to small-game hunters in January and February. For Glen Solomon this means two months of intense hog hunting.

Deer season has about run out. It turned into a job — slapping 4 a.m. alarm clocks and lugging climbers around — didn't it? Ready to get that predatory surge of adrenaline pumping through those hunting veins again? It's time to hunt hogs. If you love to hunt and have never stalked hogs, you are missing out on some exciting adventures. If you are unsure about how to locate and then properly hunt for hogs, read on!

I only hunt WMAs, which receive some pretty high hunter pressure, so to be successful I have to enact my tactics to the extreme. I walk long distances, hunt all day, do whatever it takes to find and kill hogs.

For the next 60 days — which ends February 28 on the last day of small-game season — I'll spend nearly 100 percent of my hunting time on WMAs. Get in the game; the number of hog-hunting opportunities abound in January and February.

To become a successful WMA hog hunter, you must possess confidence and the willingness to walk your tail off. Read the article "Walking Miles for Chickasawhatchee Hogs" that was published in *GON*'s January 2006 issue. *GON* editor Brad Gill and I walked more than 10 miles before we found hogs, but it resulted in two dead pigs one morning.

*Glen Solomon of Hazlehurst with a Chickasawhatchee WMA hog that he shot in November 2006 after walking more than 10 miles to find fresh sign.*

With confidence and a good pair of walking boots, you're now ready to hunt. I'm going to provide you some tips and physical maneuvers to engage your WMA hog-hunting battle plan.

**1.** Own a handheld GPS and know how to mark, locate and project waypoints. If you don't have one, get one. It's one of the most helpful hunting investments you can own.

**2.** Acquire a WMA map from the check station or Internet. Make sure the map has a compass and a distance gauge on it. The compass and distance readings in accordance with your GPS will be important to finding hogs.

Study how all the roads and drainages (creeks and rivers) or any isolated swamps are positioned on the map. Hogs and drainages go hand in hand like antlers and rubs. Pay special attention to the most remote sections, meaning the farthest from any road or access trail. This is your optimum chance for finding a hog sanctuary on a pressured WMA. Also, look for sharp turns in creeks or rivers which may create a peninsula-type area surrounded by water. Hogs feel safe in these type areas (if thick cover is present), in which water provides several avenues of escape. A lot of hunters tend to stick to a fixed course along a waterway, failing to swing out to check these small hotspots.

You'll also want to check the perimeters on the WMA. Are there any natural barriers (busy highways, rivers, lakes, populated areas, etc.), cropfields or hunting clubs? Hunting clubs will be magnets because of feeders and food plots, and cropfields speak for themselves. These sites will be raided at night, and hopefully the hogs are using security cover on the WMA.

*Hog trails often lead to swamps or sloughs. Glen says this is a great indication that the hogs are resting on a nearby island or tussock. Be prepared to don some hip waders or plan to drip dry on the other side.*

**3.** When I start cold on a WMA, I start eliminating ground. I'll drive all the roads and become familiar with them in relation to the map. I exclude parking areas, open fields or pastures and any areas showing clues of hunter frequency (boot tracks, tire treads, toilet paper in the nearby brush, etc). Eliminate the "pretty spots" you see from the road; everyone else sees them, too. I eliminate hunter-access trails for at least a quarter mile in and all land within a quarter mile of a driveable road.

**4.** While driving the roads, look for fresh hog tracks crossing the road or fresh rootings on or near the ditches or shoulders. Most of this sign will be night traffic, since hogs can range for many miles each night; however, it's a starting point for finding hogs. Mark this sign on your GPS.

On the map look for the nearest swamp or security cover. This cover will range from bottomland swamps, clearcuts (new or overgrown), big open pinelands, or young pine plantations. Overgrown swamp clearcuts and young pine plantations interwoven with tall grass, briars, bamboo and vines are a staple for a good hog hideout.

If you think the nearest cover is a good ways from the sign you're seeing from the road, you can look at your WMA map and project which direction to travel. Using the map's distance gauge and compass you can read how far you must travel to reach the bedding area. Log that waypoint into your GPS and strike a trail.

You won't always find hog sign while driving WMA roads. When this happens, park the truck, put on your hiking boots and get to work.

**5.** Follow drainages. Hogs will always relate to drainage systems. Wet-weather ponds or backup water from flooded lakes are good, too.

When I find fresh sign, I slow my OTG (on-the-ground) hunting way down — and pay close attention to wind direction as I put on a slow stalk following the fresh sign.

Look for fresh rootings and tracks. If you see rooted areas with new and old sign mixed, that's good news because hogs are returning with regularity. If you see a wallow with muddy water in it, hogs have just left and may be nearby. At wallow sites, "itchy" hogs make mud rubs on surrounding trees, (especially on outgoing trails) which is a definite indicator of what size hogs are in the area. Also look for worn and polished pine trees (tar rubs) which indicate frequent use in a core area. Mark all fresh sign on your GPS.

*John "Longjon" Bookhardt, of Snipesville, with an Ocmulgee WMA hog. John, who hunts with the author, hunts exclusively with a longbow.*

When hunting hogs, I'm always trying to stay with the freshest sign possible. I've found fresh hog sign in some areas as small as just a couple of acres, but I've also followed sign for more than a mile. I'll try to unweave the direction the fresh sign is going, hopefully closing in on some mini-dozers while their noses are still buried. If I feel I'm in an area that's so fresh that I'm seeing wet leaves or I can smell the hogs, I start zig-zagging or making figure eights until I find them.

If I don't see hogs, and the fresh feeding sign plays out, the hogs are likely in another area bedded up.

**6.** Once I've covered all the fresh sign and I've seen no hogs, I'll look for a narrow, well-trodden trail leaving the area. These trails will have a direct destination to the hogs' feeding or bedding area. Mark the trail with your GPS.

When hunting down these trails you won't always be able to play the wind. You can't circle around if you don't know the destination. You may have to bust these hogs this time to know where to be next time.

When following hog trails for the first time, I enter into speed-trolling mode. If the breeze is light, you may get to settle those crosshairs before you are detected. Keep that head spinning and eyes scanning. Hunted animals have learned that most humans walk constantly, STOP IT! If you can, in noisy cover, emit low yelps like a turkey hen. I've literally almost stepped on hogs when crashing through noisy cover by making brief pauses and "friends of the forest" vocalizations. Since hogs usually feed in groups, they must have thought I was one of their own. Be prepared to shoot quickly, in case they are waiting on your debut to be sure. If you barely see them first or make eye contact simultaneously, squat or drop to your knees quickly to break your profile. Humans are the only predators that tall in the woods, and you will be surprised as to how many animals will stick around for a shot.

*Look for fresh sign like this muddy hog wallow.*

**7.** If the trail you are following leads into an area of water, you can bet those hogs are bedding on small islands or tussocks. That's when I don some hip waders or plan to drip dry on the other side. Like I said, I hunt extreme!

Oh yeah, mark this on the GPS.

I'll enter a bedding area only after I've tried to catch them in their feeding areas. If you bust them here, you may have to wait a spell for them to return. Sometimes the hogs will be primarily nocturnal in their feeding jaunts, and you will have no other choice. Find trails going into these "jungles" and ease in, working the wind. Some of these areas, once inside, will have more open pockets to stalk more quietly. If it is a primary bedding area, there will be a maze of narrow "rabbit-like" trails. Likely, these will be your only avenues to traverse through it with any reasonable attempts for success. Be prepared for stinging briars and body-snaring vines. Limb shears will come in real handy. Some places you may even have to crawl for quite a ways. It's extreme hunting — you're in their world now.

*Rooting sign makes it easy to see where hogs have been recently feeding.*

**8.** I've been telling you to keep marking all areas with the GPS. When you get done hunting for the day, mark fresh sign, bedding areas, travel routes and any hog sightings on the map. With all these key elements marked, a "battle plan" should unfold beneath your eyes making you a more prepared and confident hunter on your next hunt.

On my first return trip I'll head to all the feeding areas, which is every place I found fresh sign. A critical step to my success is that on my return hunt I always take a different route to the sign than the ones I have previously taken. Your GPS will be very useful here. By taking a different route, you'll often discover that hogs are utilizing a different stretch of woods, one where you can catch them up feeding in the middle of the day. The trick is to leave no stone unturned.

In August 2004, me and fellow hog slayer, Don Wood, of Waynesville, while "Hunting on the Fly," hunted for two weeks on a local WMA and killed 11 hogs. We marked all bedding and feeding, travel and kill areas and created a where-to hog map. This August we returned with our mapped-out battle plan. Even two years later the hogs were using the same areas. We hunted four mornings, and we approached all our marked areas on the map from different directions. We killed 13 hogs and passed up others thus proving how marking areas on a map and accessing them from a different area can prove successful time and time again.

With the GPS, you will be more efficient and productive in your search, hitting only proven and probable areas instead of burning time on wasted ground. By going directly from one "hog waypoint" to another, you will remain in the strike zone longer, making crossing paths with Porky inevitable.

On most WMAs, hogs may be hunted in January and February with small-game weapons if small-game season is open. Along with .22s, you can hunt WMA hogs with muzzleloaders and archery equipment. Before hunting hogs on any WMA, refer to the hunting regulations to make sure the area is open to hog hunting.

Take the WMA challenge. You will become a better hunter while enjoying an endless amount of hunting land. Thank God for we are blessed with an abundance of outdoor opportunities in Georgia.

Hunting on the Fly

# Chapter 11
## All Hogs and No Squirrels on Opening Day

By Glen Solomon

A blessed day for this squirrel opener. Four hours in the woods, zero squirrels seen, wow! Still a hog magnet though, I can't get away from em! Got to woods a little late, due to hitting the snooze button and McDonald's being a lot sloooow this morning. Several miles back into the WMA, I finally made it after an hour & 11-minute drive. Woods are bright now but no worry, stumbling blocks could just be the LORD working his magic, timing and placement. I learned long ago not to fret, finish the race.

First spot, I found some fresh hog tracks at the road where I entered. I figured I'd try for squirrels first and back-track the hog sign while doing so. I'd rather have a mess of squirrels. Even though the sign meandered all over the plain, it was easy to follow as there was a hard shower last night. Finally, the sign funneled down to one good trail, coming up on a high ridge in the swamp. Here that would only be a couple or 3 feet, but enough to be above the webwork of small sloughs and bogs. The route on that ridge was eaten up with sign! Along one side, the ridge was turning into a grassy tupelo bog. The right was a slough growing in size as it neared an oxbow lake. Farther down the slough, I came upon an old silted up beaver dam crossing it, or it could've once been part of an old logging road a hundred years ago. Anyhow, it was a MAJOR CROSSING. The crossing. Immediately, I downloaded in the GPS for the next August. It wasn't long before I come upon a group of hogs heading my way, a boar, a sow and five shoats. The sow looked good having most of her weight back on. Dead center of the shoulder, PAP! 30 yd run plowing dirt all the way, then FLOP! Quartered up and headed back to the truck, 4/10 of a mile away.

*Glen with the spotted sow hog.*

A sharp knife, backpack and ice bags come in handy. This was definitely a different group coming up behind the others. Go the opposite direction, and I still can't get away from 'em. A couple set of tracks of those at the road earlier were huge, so I definitely knew it was another group. They'll be bedding along the river in a viney run along behind the willows. That's where they usually are, until after a weekend or two of feists running around.

Less than a half mile away is a hunting club which explains why these hogs looked so healthy. Ain't much in the plain now besides worms and roots and some scattered wild grapes. From past chases and this morning, I finally pieced their route in this part of the WMA. They run to the hunt clubs at night, head back into the WMA, follow up behind a certain oxbow lake, hit the crossing dam on the feeder slough, run the high ridge until it plays out, then any of several directions onto a very wide open plain but coming together at a slight bend on the drive road. They cross into the next block, hit a major wallow area, follow a long green strip, crossing an access trail into a fringe block along the river where they lay up. Now I have a complete set of GPS coordinates along this route. Sounds all good, but this spot will only be good for a very short spell. Hunting pressure is on the way. Glad the 15th, opening day, was on a weekday!

Back to the truck. Drank a gallon of water and hit BLAST on the A/C. Headed to the other end of the WMA to check on some pines that squirrels like to cut in. 300 yards down a dim access trail, 20 yds to my left pilfering along was a plump lil boar hog. Bless his little heart, picking up juicy muscadines 'n all. Center shoulder, PAAP! 30 yds later, PLOP! Healthiest hog all summer, had an inch of fat in some places. Still no squirrels. 4 hours in da woods and several miles accessing roads by truck, not even 1 squirrel sighted.

*Glen with a nice WMA brown boar hog.*

At least the LORD granted me 2 pork-ticipation awards! Also, when I got back to the kiosk, I noticed a big piece of trash on the ground. Picked it up, wrote on it was "free map." Unrolled, a large kiosk map of Big Hammock. Apparently, they put a new one up and left this one for me to find. Cool! Amen!

# Chapter 12
## All Alone Hunting for Fort Stewart Hogs

By Glen Solomon
Published by *GON* on August 2, 2012.

**Author shoots 525 pounds of pork in one day.**

*This is one of three Fort Stewart hogs Glen Solomon, of Hazlehurst, killed on a recent Saturday. This one weighed 225 pounds.*

A tornado hit Fort Stewart! Well, not really. The whirlwind that swept through on a recent weekend was actually me. Being I haven't been in the woods for nearly six months due to work travel, I hit Fort Stewart with a vengeance. Thank God there was somewhere in my part of the state open to hunt this time of year. I was about to blow a gasket!

Entering the woods at 10:30 a.m., I followed scattered pig sign in from a road crossing made the night before. Staying on the freshest sign, I looped and made figure-8s until I discovered where they had lain up for the day. They were in a head-high gallberry thicket situated in the inside turn of a ty-ty branch. As I stalked along the transition between the two, I caught some movement to my right. It was the top of a gallberry bush wiggling. Just an armadillo or a little bird bugging, I thought, as I eased forward.

Nope! It was two solid-black gilts rooting around as they eased out of their sanctuary for the day. I chose the plumpest of the two and squeezed the trigger on about a 40-pounder. My first kill of the season! The other ran back into the thicket. Waiting a few minutes, I eased into the thicket. I heard the other give a few low grunts, as if it was asking, "Is that you?" I let out a couple of low grunts and shuffled my feet.

The shoat came within 15 feet and paused, catching my scent. I could see black through the thick stems, but I couldn't tell which end I was looking at. A little voice said, "Pass." There was no need to ruin a good hunt searching for a badly hit animal or destroying meat, even though I knew the short mag could've punched through.

At 4 p.m. and 7/10 of a mile from the truck, I called it a day. I wanted to get back and prepare for my first full day of hunting the next day, a day I'd been dreaming about for months. I wanted to relax and make some new memories along the way.

The next morning, I began walking at 6:30 a.m. and didn't stop until 8:30 that evening. I signed in and out of 10 areas, walked between 1/2- to 1 1/2-mile loops in each one. I burned nearly a tank of gas in four different counties, hunting and driving completely around Fort Stewart. I had turned ravenous for some time in God's Great Outdoors after six months of work and stress in a jungle of concrete and steel.

The spirit in me was driving, "Never give up, never give up!" My body was tired and aching, but I kept going. It was going to be a hog or dark, whichever came first. The last part of the day was used figuring out some hogs that were cutting corners in four different blocks that encompassed nearly 2 square miles. It finally came together at 7:55 p.m. as I met a group of seven hogs, trotting across a burned pine flat heading to an evening area of wallows. I picked out the largest, about 70 pounds, and tickled the trigger. Boom! Right in its tracks. It was another fat gilt. Unbelievable! Another fine piece of meat.

Woo-Wee! The weekend of the tornado! Thank you, Jesus! I dropped to my knees and raised both hands high in the air as I praised Him. Only He and I knew how much I really needed that full day of hunting.

It was totally amazing. I spent the day on an area that encompasses more than 250,000 acres without seeing another hunter in the woods or passing any on its many miles of dirt roads. Even more amazing was that every area I checked into had no other hunters signed in, and on a Saturday to top that!

I had put in a round-trip time of 18 hours (driving, hunting and butchering), a tank of gas, a whole bottle of 100 percent DEET, two ThermaCELL cylinders, two sets of GPS batteries, 8 miles of wading swamps and pushing through palmettos and gallberry thickets in three different counties, eight embedded seed ticks, and my body was polka-dotted with chigger bites. All in one day!

Georgia is very lucky to have Fort Stewart as an outdoor getaway, somewhere you can hunt year-round. There is nowhere else in Georgia on public land where the general public can pursue feral hogs all year. Note: During turkey season hog hunting is only open in archery-only areas.

As I spent a day and a half hunting, I do admit it felt kind of weird toting my .270 WSM during the summer. Of course, weapon-type requirements will change as other types of game seasons come and go on Fort Stewart.

You could never hunt all this land, which is located in five counties: Bryan, Evans, Liberty, Long and Tattnall. There will always be a greener pasture around the corner. There will always be another deep hog wallow, another hidden ridge of white oaks, an island in the swamp, a travel corridor along a drainage, or an oasis of wild blueberries on a pine flat completely surrounded by a ty ty swamp.

When you hunt Fort Stewart, make sure you bring a GPS or compass. Some of these blocks are immense, ranging from several hundred to several thousand acres in size. Before writing this article, I hunted a total of five days and never saw another person or a vehicle. On some main roads, my tire tracks were the only ones for several days.

Here's the best advice I can give you. Don't try to learn the whole area at one time. Pick one for the day and learn it. Most blocks here will have hogs on them at times based on food sources and pressure. I have a lot of success at times in areas of minimal sign because hogs are very nomadic, constantly transitioning to different food sources. Sometimes you have to stay ahead of them. Lone boars also stay on the move looking for hot sows, and you are apt to see one at any time anywhere.

While you are out there, mark some good deer spots for the upcoming season. I can hardly wait to climb 30 feet up a particular slash pine, overlooking a dense tangle of vines and fallen trees inside of which is hidden, well... ain't tellin' ya!

My best day was the following Saturday. I bagged a 125-lb. sow and two boars that went 175 and 225 pounds. I saw at least 15 deer, an additional dozen or so hogs, three bushels of squirrels, five coyotes, two raccoons, two rabbits, a bobcat, and I lost count of the turkeys. I also saw 15 swallow-tailed kites in one group circling above the trees (which are very rare), gopher tortoises, and a 5-foot alligator in a small flat pond. It was a very enjoyable and blessed day indeed.

You're probably going to laugh when I tell you how I oftentimes make my decision on which areas I'm going to hunt. I have a coffee can that has labeled and laminated pieces of paper for all the hunting areas. I shake the can, my wife pulls out one, and that's where I go for the day. If it's not an open area for that day, she'll draw again. I call it "Shake 'n Bacon."

*Glen had a good day at Ft. Stewart.*

It doesn't matter what she draws out. There is hog sign in every block out there, and there's always something to see, learn and enjoy. I've always been good at speed-scouting and eliminating. I can't stand not knowing every inch of an area, so to speak. I came up with the Shake 'n Bacon method or I would pull my hair out with so much land to choose from.

However, you determine where you're going to hunt, the most typical way to get on hogs quickly is to drive around the block and find the freshest tracks or wallows along the edges. Right after a rain is when I love to drive around. The darkened sand and red clay smoothed by the rain will really illuminate tracks. Follow their sign. If you lose it, start gridding off the area, paying special attention to the thicker cover and wet areas. For extra hunting tips, go to www.gon.com, click on "Hunting," then "Hog" and scroll down to "Summer Sausage Run."

*"Shake 'n Bacon."*

If you decide to hunt hogs at Fort Stewart this month, definitely bring a ThermaCELL, high-volume DEET, a GPS/compass, map, extra shirts because you will sweat and plenty of water. Also, because meat will spoil quickly in the summer, bring a game cart or a backpack if you want to quarter up your hog in the woods. I sleeve my meat in the 20-lb. bags from the ice machine before tossing it in my pack. If I ever see any bags hanging on the chute arm where people leave them, I stop and pick them up. I also use them for freezer bags, and they are long enough to double over. If you cart out, there is a cleaning station by the Pass and Permit Office.

In closing, I apologize to any of the regulars who hunt here for bringing to light what an overwhelming abundance of outdoor opportunities that abound at Fort Stewart/HAAF. There was a time when I would've been selfish and kept it a secret, too, but I feel it is far more important to promote our hunting heritage. If I can excite someone to start hunting or to hog hunt for the first time, or even to re-ignite a passion for someone who may has stopped hunting because of lease prices or smaller crowded WMAs, I will then feel I have done my duty helping my fellow outdoorsman. Anyway, there is plenty of elbow room, and I sure left a bunch of hogs behind.

My freezers and heart are full. Is yours? God bless, and start making tracks!

The military changes regulations from time to time regarding recreational opportunities on Ft. Stewart. As this is written the GA DNR instructions are to reference the website https://ftstewart.isportsman.net and follow the instructions given there regarding the regulations.

# Chapter 13
## Hog Attacks Hunter On Chickasawhatchee WMA

By Glen Solomon
Published by *GON* February 2014

Did I miss? A moment earlier 110 yards away stood a fat Chickasawhatchee WMA swamp doe stomping her foot in my direction. Quartering toward me slightly, I opted to take the shot as I knew broadside wasn't going to happen. Before the shot's echo silenced from within the mile-deep swamp, she had streaked from view with two others, white flags bounding among the aligning cypresses and tupelos. As I neared where she had been standing, I saw the draw that had them feeding there. A huge chestnut oak was raining down the last of its acorns from the previous day's winds. The ground underneath the drip line of the oak was solid mud, churned from the multitude of deer and hog tracks. Being partially color-blind, I surprisingly found the blood trail quickly, due to its glisten of wetness. I found her only 50 yards away piled up against an old cypress log. It took a little longer than normal to field-dress since I had to pause and let two more does work around me, heading to their sanctuary for the day. It was probably the other two from earlier, calming down and waiting for the matriarch doe that had once been their lead. A 200-yard boot-sinking drag was next in order. I would then have her in place on a dim path that would make the game cart very useful, which was in my truck nearly 3/4 of a mile away. I would have to walk past a friend, David Rodriguez, of Homestead, Fla., whom I had dropped off at another hot feed area on the way in.

Nearing David on my return trip for the cart, I rested upon an old logging relic left from the early 1900s. My little break would allow him a little more sit time. Aside from the usual scattered railcar axles used on the old trams, this relic was unique. It appeared to be a log winch that was used to retrieve trees across the deeper parts of the swamp. Sitting on a large frame the size of a pickup, it had huge cogged gears and even a radiator. Sure is a lot of history in this swamp.

*Old timey log winch abandoned in the swamp.*

Years ago, I discovered an old unmarked cemetery near Spring Creek on the other side of the WMA that dated back to the late 1800s. It was nestled in a small grove of live oaks in the middle of a pine plantation. Since then the timber has been thinned, and I'm sure many are aware of it now. I motioned to David in redneck sign language that I was going to get the game cart and for him to stay put and get some more air time. No need for him to walk back out and then right back in at that distance. He was in a sweet spot, and I was confident that something was going to feed there sometime today. Usually, unless disturbed or you get winded, deer or hog will return at midday on a hot food source. Back at the truck I grabbed the game cart but ditched all my non-essential gear and excess outer clothing. I decided to leave my rifle, being I had my handgun. This turned out to be a mistake. Mr. Murphy's Law whispered something in my ear about carrying the rifle back in. A lot could happen in a 6/10 of a mile walk.

I did see a doe two-thirds of the way back in but would've passed anyway. She was standing near the same scrape we had seen a 130- to 140-class buck while heading in that morning before daylight. Fifteen yards away in full beam, we all observed each other with mouths wide open for a full 10 seconds before he bounded away Wow!

The last 100 yards before David would come into view, I slowed to a snail's pace. We made eye contact, 11:45 and nothing sighted yet. Maybe I should've given him longer. Rolling ahead and 50 yards from his tree, three black tanks suddenly appeared. Hogs! I dropped the cart's handle and pulled my pistol from its holster. Before I could cycle a round in the chamber, David's .308 barked, Boom! Two of the hogs ran in one direction, and the one he hit went another direction, plowing its chin along the ground with front legs folded beneath it. I saw David swing the rifle, Boom! Boom! He dropped a huge boar on the run. I looked back to the first hog he shot, and it was back up and running in the opposite direction plowing the ground again. It flopped a couple times and took off again. Wait a minute, three death runs? Even with the front axle knocked out from under it, it was pushing a furrow with its snout 20 yards or more each time. I went toward the hog as it stood up, and it seemed to shake it off. I then noticed what was going on. David had only hit the hog in the lower leg. As I neared within 5 yards, the hog had gained some balance and began to trot away. Mind you, a three-legged hog can still move pretty quick, and boy was I ever fixing to find out! I aimed behind the shoulder and fired two quick rounds from my XD .40. Instead of falling, the hog turned and charged me. While running away, I unloaded on it (I only had six rounds in the gun). I stopped running when the hog fell to its knees. Geez! Sucker about caught me! With a good distance between me and the hog, I motioned toward David to shoot, but he was still sitting up there doing nothing. I walked back within 5 feet of the still-alive hog as it was still kneeled down. I then noticed one of the back-handed shots had blown the top of its skull slam off. I could even see what appeared to be the bottom of its cranial cavity with half the brain missing. I knew the first two rounds in the torso had connected. I looked back at David in the tree. Why isn't he getting down? I hollered, "Hurry up and get down, I ain't got no more bullets!" I know he could still see the hog was still alive. The hog then stood back up and charged again! I barely made it to a tree that would at least give me a little break and have something between us. As it turned, I picked up a large limb and slapped it across the head. The next three to four minutes I was beating it with whatever I could pick-up, but everything was half-rotten. I was trying to stall it until David could get down and approach for a killing shot. All the while, I figured it would topple over any second from the earlier injuries. Wrong! While side-stepping, jumping, kicking, hollering for quite a spell and nearly getting bit or cut several times, it took forever for David to start getting out of the tree. After me and the hog wound up on each side of a large tree, I noticed David finally climbing down. The hog was still breathing good and still holding its head high. Please hurry! I then realized I had my skinning knife on my side. If I can peek around the tree, stretch and come up and over the hog, maybe I can stab it in the lungs on the opposite side. Well, that Rambo idea worked. Bad thing was, the hog gained momentum again and chased me around the tree before falling to its front knees again. Okay, maybe that's it now. I hope so, one of the best and favorite knives I've ever owned is still in its side. I couldn't pull it out because of the gut hook feature on it. Anyhow, I didn't have time for a second stab.

I looked over and noticed slow-poke was near the bottom of the tree. I looked back at the hog and noticed it was trying to regain its balance again. No! Hurry, David! What can I do? The hog is fixing to leave and I'm tired of playing hopscotch with a hog. I then noticed a large limb with a smaller and greener pointed end. Maybe, just maybe, I can stob it in the head where the top of its skull used to be and knock it out, kill it, paralyze it, something. Stob is not misspelled, it's a redneck word. Stab only befits something sharp. I eased forward with my primal spear. Please don't charge again. I raise it over my head, bulls-eye, uh oh!

I'm sure glad I didn't let go of the stick. Here I go running backward getting pushed by a monster hog with a stick in the top of its head and my knife still wagging in its side like a dog's tail. I finally made it to a tree to sidestep behind. The hog stopped and turned. David appeared. Neck shot. Finally.

Upon quartering the hog, I discovered the two hollow-point PMC rounds did not expand, even after penetrating nearly a 2-foot-wide hog. One zipped through. The other fell in my hand as I peeled the opposite hide back.

*David Rodriguez of Homestead Florida with two hogs taken in this story. The lower one is the sow that attacked the author.*

Both hogs were easily heavier than 300 pounds. We flipped the cart on its side and both of us strained to get the boar on first. We pulled like a mule team for only a few yards before giving up. Out of the muddier areas, the wheels were still sinking a couple inches in the soft earth making progress of this heavy load futile. Maybe on a hard pan road, but not here.

Plan B. The first trip was with the deer and both climbers. After this circus, it wouldn't be of any use to re-climb here any time soon. Five sonic booms of magnum rifles, six rounds unloaded from a handgun, half a dozen or more large limbs slapping and breaking, teeth snapping and popping and grunting from the hog, me hollering and perhaps a couple of those mysterious girly screams, talking aloud afterward, Praising Him, etc. will wind this spot up. Too, quartering the hogs here would also add to the pheromone mountain of scent in this once quiet and undisturbed pristine swamp.

We returned with large backpacks, ice bags and the cart. Glad I did! Just the eight quarters and backstraps was a load itself. We both had to pull. When flipping the boar over for a photo, its snout fell across my boot. Dadgum. Its long-curled tusk cut a big hole in the top of my brand-new rubber boots. First day I ever wore'em. I later discovered after washing all the mud, blood, and hog slobber off, that the other boot also had a penetrating cut. From dancing in the sticks or the big sow's teeth? Believe me, she had some nice ones, too. I really don't know, but I do remember feeling the close brush of the hog against me at least three times. One of those close calls seemed to go in slow motion before impact, strong eye-to-eye contact, where it seemed she definitely had me caught. Thanks for the hand on me from above for placing that barrier. This hunt was one of the most fast-paced exciting, dangerous and physical-exerting hunts I've ever been on.

Our camping/hunting party ended up with nine deer and the two hogs. We also enjoyed a few squirrels I shot earlier in the week during my scouting. They were a real treat for my two friends who have never hunted or eaten any. Someone missed a big step in their hunting childhood. There will be squirrel hunting in their future. They seemed to be excited about it for next year.

*The author with about a dozen squirrels taken for camp meat.*

# Epilogue
## A Celebration of the Life of Glen Solomon

By Bill Prince
This eulogy was spoken at Glen's memorial service on
August 18, 2019.

Welcome to this gathering where you will be comforted in your loss of Glen Solomon and we will celebrate Glen's life.

*"I will lift up mine eyes unto the hills, from whence cometh my help. ₂My help cometh from the LORD, which made heaven and earth. ₃He will not suffer thy foot to be moved: he that keepeth thee will not slumber. ₄Behold, he that keepeth Israel shall neither slumber nor sleep. ₅The LORD is thy keeper: the LORD is thy shade upon thy right hand. ₆The sun shall not smite thee by day, nor the moon by night. ₇The LORD shall preserve thee from all evil: he shall preserve thy soul. ₈The LORD shall preserve thy going out and thy coming in from this time forth, and even for evermore,"* (Psalm 121, KJV).

Let us pray. In the name of Jesus, with thanksgiving, with praise, for this place, for this people, asking for blessing on this assembly, on these activities, asking for comfort by your blessed Holy Spirit, as we celebrate the life of Glen Solomon, breathe on us O God. May our celebration be pleasing unto you.

Ms. Cindy, Corey & Erica, Candace & Jeffery, other family, we are here to comfort each other. I have known Glen several years. Met at Googe's Store. I had read his stories in *GON* and knew of him but recently, we developed a closer association. We shared a love for writing about our experiences. Sixteen days ago, Glen and I worshiped together at a gathering of Christian men in this town. There we heard a great inspiring biblical message for men. When the speaker made an altar call, Glen was one of the first to kneel in reverence to God and I joined him. We both prayed prayers that were heartfelt of thanksgiving, praise and commitment to live to please God. We stayed at the altar until the program moved on, and then some.

During our fishing trips, we shared constantly. With Glen and me it was somewhat of a battle as to who had the floor. I did not mind yielding to Glen because he had something to say. There is a difference between having to say something and having something to say, and Glen did have something to say. I learned something from Glen every time he spoke. Some tall tales have been told off the bench at Googe's Store, but I have not seen any reason to doubt any of Glen's reports, and he had the pictures and videos to back them up. Glen was accomplished as a sportsman, husband, father, writer, videographer and friend. Glen would share some wit and wisdom and then chuckle. He told me of men who had come into his camp with what he called a potty mouth and said he had to ask them to tone it down, and if they didn't, there were excluded in future camps. Glen didn't go along with potty mouth.

The most important information we shared was about our faith. Glen loved Jesus as I do, and we both talked about our faith. Men talk about what's important to them when they get relaxed and have time to share. Glen spoke of faith and family, Ms. Cindy and Corey, the places and happenings concerning hunting and fishing. We also talked about words, their selection and use, and sentence structure. We talked about how we had to re-write at times to avoid what we didn't like, prepositional phrases in formal writing in particular.

Glen had a testimony of faith in Christ alone as Savior. Glen understood that man is a sinner and God is Holy. Sinful men cannot enter into the presence of Holy God – in fact Glen knew that NO sin can enter into the presence of Holy God. Glen knew that God had made a way for us to go to our heavenly home when our life here ends. There must be an experience which prepares us for that homegoing. God sent Jesus, His only begotten son, to Calvary's cross, where He suffered and died, shed His Holy sinless blood, then was buried, and resurrected, and ascended into heaven where he was waiting on Glen. Glen and I shared some of our testimonies, enough for me to know – Glen had faith, believed in what Christ did for him, trusted in the blood of Jesus for salvation and had a relationship based on this faith with Holy God. That's why I can say with confidence that Glen is in heaven. Where is Glen you ask? What is heaven like? Ms. Cindy, Corey, Erika, Candace – others, Heaven is a happy place.

*"In your presence is the fullness of joy, at your right hand are pleasures, forevermore,"* (Psalm 16:11, KJV).

Being happy has to do with your happenings. When your happenings are happening the way you want them to happen, you are happy. Glen is happy and in a happy place. Heaven is a healthy place.

*"He will wipe away every tear from their eyes. There will be no more death or mourning or crying or pain. For the former things are passed away,"* (Revelation 21:4, KJV).

I awakened about 3 AM this morning having left the TV on playing gospel music from Youtube. Dottie Rambo was singing a song she wrote, "Tears Will Never Stain the Streets of that City." I thought immediately of Glen and where he was. Glen is in a happy place and Glen is in a healthy place. Also, heaven is a holy place.

*"Now I know the Lord saved His anointed, He will hear him from his holy heaven with the saving strength of his right hand,"* (Psalm 20:6, KJV).

God is omniscient. He sees and know all. I like to think about it like this, God can see everything but Glen's sins because they are covered by the blood of Jesus. Glen is in a holy place. Heaven is a home place. Rejoice family and friends, we can celebrate Glen's life. He had 3 homes. I guess you could say 4 homes for Glen and count all the WMA's in Georgia as one of his homes. 596 Pat Dixon Rd was his family home. He would say to me when I asked where we would meet when going fishing, "Meet me at the barn."

That's 596 Pat Dixon Rd. Glen had his faith home, Lighthouse Christian Fellowship, here where we stand, he would meet with his faith family. Glen had his future home which is now his forever home. Heaven above. He is now in his place of permanence. There will be no more moves for Glen. Happy, Healthy, Holy, and Home. We must be encouraged, though we miss him, be comforted. Glen wants you all to come be with him. Pastor Ty will be sharing with you and giving anyone here who needs the assurance of salvation an opportunity to prepare to go be with Glen when your time comes leave this world. I thank you for the privilege and honor eulogizing my friend, Glen Solomon.

Bill Prince August 18, 2019 Hazlehurst, Jeff Davis, Georgia Permission to share granted. I hope this is a fair representation of what I said that day, written from memory with a few notes.

Hunting on the Fly

198

Glen Solomon

Lightning Source UK Ltd.
Milton Keynes UK
UKHW021022030120
356279UK00005B/92/P

9 781951 497125